COUNTRY SCHOOL
MEMORIES

To Ma,
remember the
good old days —
Love,
Bonnie

Other books by Bonnie Hughes Falk

FORGET-ME-NOT
POTPOURRI OF NOSTALGIA

COUNTRY SCHOOL MEMORIES

Designed and Compiled by
Bonnie Hughes Falk

Illustrated by
Nancy Delage Huber

Library of Congress Catalog Card Number:
86-091104

ISBN 0-9614108-1-7

Published by BHF Memories Unlimited,
3470 Rolling View Court, White Bear Lake, MN 55110

Distributed by Adventure Publications,
P.O. Box 269, Cambridge, MN 55008

Printed in the United States of America

*To Mother and Dad,
both of whom attended
a country school.*

CONTENTS

INTRODUCTION

- *The aroma of a one-room schoolhouse on a crisp winter morning, with the stove glowing red hot*
- *The smell of wet mittens drying on the wood-burning stove*
- *The desks with the inkwell in the right-hand corner*
- *The cold treks to the "little house" out back*
- *The "everyone share" drinking dippers*
- *The "syrup pail" lunches*
- *The cry of "Anti Over"*

Memories — that's what this book is all about. It is a collection of "Country School Memories" from individuals who experienced the one-room school as a teacher or pupil.

The schoolhouse was the center of the rural community for many years — woven into the lives of all it touched. A special kind of education was provided there, and the character-building principles taught and learned linger on in the memories of all it served.

I felt the one-room school was too much a part of our heritage to be forgotten, so I contacted individuals throughout Minnesota and neighboring states and asked them to send me recollections of their country school days. From the many delightful letters I received, I chose excerpts depicting various aspects of country school life. My only regret is that due to space and duplication of material, I was unable to use all of the information I received. The names of the contributors, along with their country school involvement, are listed in the Acknowledgments in the back of the book.

I hope this book will recreate the flavor of the one-room school and the rural communities it served, and that you will enjoy reliving memories from the past.

Bonnie Hughes Falk

THE ONE-ROOM
SCHOOLHOUSE

THE ONE-ROOM SCHOOLHOUSE

I started first grade in 1917 in a typical country school. Like all country schools (which seem to have all used the same plans), it had one room, with three windows on each side which let in all the light we had. There was nothing but the sun for illumination, and on gloomy days we couldn't study. Each school had a cloakroom in front and a coal shed in the back. There was some variation here. Some had both in front, and occasionally the school had a shed separate from the schoolhouse, which made the teacher's work harder. Each school had a stove. In my first school this was in the back. Children in the front rows were often cold and those near the stove got too warm. I remember we huddled near the stove on very cold days.

Most schools had a teacher's desk, a set of maps, a globe that was suspended from the ceiling, and pictures of Washington and Lincoln. They also had a pail and a dipper for water, a wash basin, a coal pail, and a broom and sweeping compound to use on the floor (to keep the dust down). Sweeping was made more difficult because the floors were made of rough boards. The desks were nailed to long boards so that the children couldn't move them around freely. Thank goodness that idea didn't last long because we had to move the whole row in order to sweep.

Times were hard in 1917 and on through the Depression. Our mothers saved every bit of paper that came into the house that had a plain back. These sheets were sewn together at the tops and used for tablets. Only the more well-to-do parents were able to buy store-bought tablets. We all had penny pencils; some of us had slates. They were noisy, but they saved on paper. Money was scarce, so the poor teacher didn't have much to work with either.

Bathroom facilities were primitive — little houses behind the schoolhouse, at least fifty feet apart. These were poorly constructed but served their purpose. I only taught in one school with indoor "restrooms," and they were not too satisfactory, as they were chemical toilets — no running water.
(Dorothea Thompson)

District 11 looked much like other schools scattered across the prairies during the period of World War I — a white frame building with a bell tower. The location was ideal — right between two lakes.

What else in Minnesota! The lake on the east side was the larger and also nearer the school. So here we dabbled in the springtime and slid down the snowy embankments and halfway across the lake in the winter.

Having an enrollment of forty pupils, we needed at least twenty double seats. It was of prime importance to get the partner you wanted for a deskmate. The size of the desk mattered very little. If it was a little small for you, it might be just right for your deskmate.
(Ingeborg Bolstad)

All of the buildings that I taught in were frame, except one which was stucco. They were cold in winter, hot in summer, and often had no screens or storm windows. Floors of wood were hard to keep up, but sweeping compound helped. Much scrubbing was required in muddy weather. Shades were in the middle of the windows, so they pulled both up and down. Lamps hung on the walls. There was no electricity. Dark days were good times for drill. At least one cloakroom was provided; in larger buildings there were two. A wash basin, pitcher for hand pouring, and a method of getting a drink was needed. We went from the common dipper, to cups from home, to paper cups, to the bubbler fountain.
(Arlie M. Klimes)

In our schoolyard there was a fairly large, grassy area with some trees in one corner. We had outdoor toilets until the building was remodeled, and then we had indoor "chemical" ones. Neither type was very "fragrant." There was a well and hand-operated pump on the east side. I recall the big round stove, which was protected by a metal sheath imprinted with scroll-like designs. We stood there to warm up after outside recess. There were always mittens, with their woolly smell, drying near the stove. There was a fence all around the yard. Later, remodeling added a basement and a kitchen.
(N. Wyelene Fredericksen)

The school building consisted of one room and an entry or hall. The school I attended as a student had a big jacket stove in the front corner of the room, a teacher's desk, wall maps, library shelves with glass front doors, a globe which hung from the ceiling on a pulley, blackboards on the walls all around the room, bulletin boards above the blackboards, and a water cooler and basin in the corner. The students each had their own cups in their desks. There were outdoor privies.

A big bell was in the belfry, with a rope to ring the bell hanging in the schoolrom. It was tempting to some children to pull that rope. When I was the teacher, I made it a rule that whenever that bell was rung, it was school time. So when someone ran by and pulled it during playtime, we all had to come in. Just once was enough and it wasn't touched again.
(Margaret Thompson Cimenski)

The school building was one large room, with an enclosed entry (too cold to be used during the winter months) and a porch. There was also a coal shed attached to the main room, as there was a coal stove near the center of the room which heated the building. There were about four windows on each side of the schoolroom, pictures of George Washington and Abraham Lincoln in the front of the room, and maps and a globe. Water had to be brought from home. One of the families would bring it in a big water can and get a small fee for hauling it. The water was placed in a big crock jar with a spigot and used for drinking, as well as for washing hands.
(Mary D. Thompson)

I had cousins on a farm near Spencer, Iowa, and they went to a country school. I visited them there while I was in the primary grades, and I was fascinated. Just a little old tumbling down school, with long seats that held two or more pupils. You always had a deskmate. There were noon lunches in tin pails, with covers to keep out the flies, etc. — like a picnic. I loved it and wanted to go to that school. Memories of that school always stayed with me.
(Elma Summers)

School district 55 was located ten miles southeast of Waseca. The building was very small, with just two windows on each side and a little entry. There was a square trapdoor in the ceiling leading to a small garret or attic. A first grader of the 1900 school year said his teacher threatened to put him up there if he would not be quiet. Needless to say, he never was put up there.
(Ruth V. Esping)

In the early years in country schools, there were no lights in the buildings; then kerosene bracket lamps were hung on the walls; then the Aladdin Wall Lamp with its bright light; and much later, electric lights. Each day a pail of water was carried from the neighbor's place to the school, sometimes by one of the older boys. The pupils used the one dipper from the water pail. Later, a water fountain with a faucet was used, and each child used his own cup.

All older school buildings were cold. The first heating stove was a square wood-burning box stove. Early in the morning on cold days the children sat around the stove studying. It was too cold in the back of the room. Later on, a circulating coal-burning furnace was installed. At one time heavy paper was put around the base of the school building and then banked with manure to help keep the cold out.
(Forrest and Ethelyn McKinley)

Some of my schools had indoor chemical toilets and oil burners. Water for drinking was carried from the well of a nearby farm, or I brought it from home. When the coal was stored in the shed, the locks would freeze from drips off the roof, so I kept salt water under the stove to thaw it out. Once, the coal was in the basement and there was about three feet of water down there. I was supposed to walk a plank from the steps to the coal. I finally refused because if I hit my head and fell, I might drown!
(Emily Sedlacek)

Winter was the hardest time in the country school. More than once the teacher didn't arrive until shortly before the students, so there was often no heat in the school. Since there was no insulation in the building, it would get very cold. We often sat around the stove until ten o'clock before starting classes. Ink would freeze in the inkwells and our lunches would freeze in the dinner pails on the shelves.
(Alice M. Jenkins)

We lived in North Dakota in the early 1900s. My three older sisters went to a sod schoolhouse. The walls of the building were very thick. The roof had a few green plants growing from it. One day I visited school. We four sisters all rode to school on one pony. Two sat behind the saddle, and Pearl, the oldest, drove the pony, with me on her lap holding onto the pommel. The distance was nearly two miles.

I remember being carried in the schoolroom by a nice teacher. She gave me a book to read and put me on the window ledge. Due to the thick walls, there was a lovely, big place to read. The floor was of wood and the sod walls were coated with a green color. A

stove in the corner of the room kept all of us warm. By the time I started school, a new wooden building replaced the sod building. This was approximately 1914 or 1915.
(Sally L. Ose)

Our schoolhouse was a wood frame building with windows on both sides — east and west. A round oak stove heated the building. We had outside privies, one for the boys and one for the girls. We used old catalogs instead of toilet paper!

In later years the schoolhouse was raised up and a basement was put under it. Two chemical toilets were added to the main floor, plus an entrance and a place to hang our coats. A small library was also added, with a garage for the teacher's car below it. In the basement, a kitchen was at one end, with a furnace, furnace room, and coal room at the other end. Electricity was also installed at that time. The new addition was used for community meetings, like Farm Bureau and 4-H, and miscellaneous parties.
(Elsie S. Fredericksen Williams)

The country school I attended was in a little town consisting of one store, which included the post office. The owners lived in the rear of the store. There were six more homes, three elevators, and the schoolhouse. It was a large one-room school, and about thirty pupils attended.

I was really too young to start school when I did, but my brother (two years older) was too afraid to go alone, so I went with him. When mother withdrew me, as Jack became acquainted, the teacher wrote to her saying that I was one of the better students and she would like to have me stay. Therefore, my brother and I remained in the same grade for the next eight years.
(Ruby Vickers)

Our schoolhouse was one room, with a lean-to for a coal bin and a cloakroom (unheated). There was a four-stall barn for horses. There were also two outbuildings labeled "boys" and "girls." One wall in the schoolroom was covered with blackboards and there was a case of roll-down maps. And as long as I can remember, there were half-worn-out erasers, and it was a special privilege to stay after school to clean them. There was also a teacher's desk, recitation bench (which didn't have to be large because enrollment was never over fourteen), a school clock, a picture of George Washington, a shelf with a large unabridged dictionary, and a picture of Sacajawea (a must in North Dakota schools). Our library was one tall bookcase. There was a table which held the water cooler, a covered Red Wing jar with a spigot on one side. Our lunch pails were empty syrup pails. There was no well so one of the big kids had to carry water from home. A few had fancy metal cups. The rest of us made cups by folding a piece of tablet paper. You had to drink fast because tablet paper soaked up quickly! There was a large stove, on which wet mittens always hung in the winter; there was always the smell of drying (or scorching) wool. Teachers had to learn to fire the blast with lignite, a smoky, sooty coal mined in western North Dakota. One had to strike a delicate balance between a fire that was too low and would go out overnight, a fire that was too hot and would burn out overnight, or a fire that was just right and properly banked so just a good shaking would get it going the next day.

For equipment we had big fat tablets with red covers (with a big 5 or 10 on them because that was what they cost), penny pencils of unpainted cedar that had no metal cuff to hold the eraser, inkwells in the desks, pen points that always seemed to scratch, and a windup phonograph (very cultural).

One of the things I remember best was the flag. It was special to all of us. The school day started with the pledge to the flag. It was a special privilege to put up the flag in the morning. At the first drop of rain on the window, hands were raised and waved frantically, with the cry of, "Teacher, teacher, it's raining." Teacher would immediately send someone out to take down the flag. It was *never* allowed to stay out in a storm, and I still cringe when I see flags drooping, neglected in the rain.
(Mae F. Hardin)

District 73, the Hill Billy School, stood small but sedate, surrounded on three sides by grain fields and on the south side by hilly pastures. A small graveled road meandered past the school, sweeping gently past to join the larger roads on either the east or the west end. I was fortunate to be the teacher of this little prairie school for three wonderful years.

Our light was provided by wall lamps with shining reflectors hung by brackets above the blackboards, thereby making four on each side of the room. This lamp light was frequently necessary during stormy or short winter days. How I would love to have one of those lamps now!

Our bathroom facilities consisted of a boys' and a girls' toilet built on either side of the big coal shed. There was a gray enameled wash basin, with a red bar of Lifebuoy soap beside it, standing on a small wooden stand in one corner of the schoolroom.

Water was carried by pails to fill the large crock fountain that stood just inside the schoolroom. This fountain had to be carefully drained each evening during cold weather; otherwise, the freezing water would cause it to crack. I was most thankful this never happened during my years at the school. I can well imagine the stir that would have been created had it been necessary to ask the school board to buy a new water fountain!

We were fortunate to have a case of large maps that could be pulled down when needed or rolled up when not in use. There was also a bookcase with a glass front that held perhaps as many as one hundred books. Lucky were the children whose parents took them to a public library. To be honest, I know of only one family who made use of the public library, so the children were very limited in their reading material.

The smallest desks were on one side of the room, the middle-sized desks in the middle of the room, and the large double desks on the outside. Our school wasn't very large — perhaps an average of fifteen or sixteen students in one year. Our smaller school, with all grades in one room, gave us the opportunity to give a lot of personal attention to each child. We knew our students very well because of the small classes.

The Sunday afternoon before opening day, I had the exciting task of making the schoolroom attractive by placing a jar of fall bittersweet on the bookcase, with a cluster of fall leaves placed casually beside it; then going about the room tacking up pictures cut from magazines. All teachers were especially fond of the homey Norman Rockwell pictures to be found on the cover of *The Saturday Evening Post*. These pictures mounted on bright pages of construction paper were highly prized for decorating the schoolroom. My last chore before leaving for my boarding place was to polish the little hand bell with my freshly ironed handkerchief, and to place it in a prominent spot on my newly acquired desk.

(Margaret Seeger Hedlund)

THE
LONG
WALK

THE LONG WALK

There were very few days when we didn't walk the two miles to and from school. When my brother got older, he made a "stoneboat," as it was called, and his pony, Bud, pulled it to take us to school when it was extremely cold. To keep warm we were made to wear long-legged underwear, which I always rolled up after arriving at school. It was a bit of a battle to get us to wear it, and there was always an argument to get my brother Sonny to wear something on his head.

I clearly remember the fear we often had of a large bull when we were walking to school. He seemed to know how afraid of him we were. He would paw the dirt and beller. We had heard that wearing red might anger him, so anything red was hidden. Many times we went way out of our way to avoid him. I can remember even crawling in the ditch to get past him.
(Mae Hanson Hughes Kjos)

The country school we attended was about one mile from our home. It became a long walk when it was cold. We were dressed well in the winter, and we were strong and had good legs then. Instead of coming to get us with horses if the weather was bad, my dad would walk across the field to meet us.

In the spring and fall the walks were fun. Several families walked together. In those days wild flowers grew abundantly along the road. All the huge machinery of today hadn't ruined the natural beauty of the countryside. Lots of woods were around our school, and we played there during recess. In the fall there were chokecherries and hazelnuts, which were fun to hunt and eat.
(Ada Ronnei Pederson)

My family lived two miles from school. My dad and near neighbors often gave us rides. We did not have a car until I was in the third or fourth grade, so the trips were made with horses. In the winter I remember the big bobsled, with straw in the bottom and blankets galore to keep us warm.

In the spring and fall when we walked to and from school, we were frightened of cows, and especially the bulls, which were in pastures along the way. Someone had told us that if we paid no

attention to them they would not bother us, so we would walk past them with our heads down, looking at the ground.
(Selma Anderson Hughes)

The years I attended a rural school as a student, we walked one and one-half miles each morning and afternoon, regardless of the weather. I loved school and never wanted to miss a day.

As we got older, we were required to do the breakfast dishes before leaving for school. My sister and I then would have to hurry. We'd run between two telephone poles, walk between the next two, and would arrive on the school ground many times as the last bell was ringing.
(Margaret Thompson Cimenski)

I remember walking to country school when it was quite cold. My brother and I had to walk one and one-half miles. One morning, even though I wore knitted wool mittens, my hands were really cold and I let the teacher know it. Then a boy took me out to the well and pumped C-O-L-D water on my hands! Eventually, they warmed up.

On cold, cold stormy days in the winter, my grandfather came to the school to get us. He had a medium-sized sled, pulled by a horse. He put a heavy blanket over me for the ride home.
(Orline Golden Foelschow)

One morning as I was walking to school, I heard a bull roaring. He was coming along the side road. If I quickened my pace, he did likewise. I saw I wouldn't be able to make it to the school, so I jumped the fence of a neighbor who lived close by. The bull came way up to the fence where I had jumped. By that time the neighbor was there to help me. I had never been able to jump a fence before and I haven't since! I guess panic got the best of me. The bull was sold the next day and I watched him go!
(Selma O. Sanvik)

Walking two and one-half miles to school involved many interesting experiences. Seeing the abundant violets and Dutchman's breeches on the side of the hill was always a thrill. While cutting across farmers' fields, the boys would tell us that a bull was coming after us. This caused us to run great distances to get ahead of the bull, which I never remember seeing.
(Margaret Jenkins)

14

In the spring and fall when the weather was nice, we walked the two and one-half miles to and from school each day. Sometimes we would get a ride with farmers from the area who came to the creamery in Cambria. In the winter parents would take turns transporting us to school. The roads weren't open after a snowstorm for two or three days sometimes, and we would go to school in a horse-drawn sleigh. It was fun to go in the sleigh, but it was also cold. My mother would heat bricks in the oven and wrap them in paper and cloth to help keep our feet warm.
(Alice M. Jenkins)

I boarded at a home one-fourth mile from the school, and even on the coldest days I walked. It was in the days before women wore slacks, and I would wrap newspaper under my hose to keep my legs from freezing. The years were 1927 - 1930.
(Ruby Vickers)

As far as walking to and from school, my experiences weren't all that enjoyable. I walked as much as three and one-half miles when the roads were impassable to cars. My clothing was so bulky that I doubt if I could have lifted my one hundred pounds back into a standing position if I had fallen down! Besides, subzero weather didn't help one iota. I have had both frozen hands and feet.

As a teacher, I enjoyed the enthusiasm of my pupils when they related what they had seen on the way to school. When one lad got his first glasses, he was happy to see that leaves on trees were actually separated. Those walks taught observance of things around us.

Riding back and forth was wonderful. One could roll down the windows and blow the cobwebs out of one's brain. This was my time to be alone — to meditate on the day to come, or to relive the day just past. I could see my day in retrospect, make plans, and become peaceful within myself. It was also very relaxing to drive home, anticipating some family activity before correcting papers.

One experience I had was during World War II, when gas and tires were rationed. No matter how I hoarded the gas, it just would not stretch. So unless someone gave me an unwanted stamp, I walked for a couple of days. A far greater handicap was the tires. One tire was cut and put over the other as a reinforcement. The Texaco station owner got tired of fixing the tires, so he called the ration board and told them that he was putting on four new tires and that they

should send him four stamps. The stamps came, and I am ever grateful to him.
(Arlie M. Klimes)

I taught my own daughter through the eight grades, taking her along to the rural schools. We drove as much as fifteen miles to school. One winter she walked ahead to see how hard the snowbanks were; then if they were hard, I'd drive my Model A Ford Coupe over the top. Because of floods one spring, we drove eighty miles a day to get to a school twelve miles away.
(Emily Sedlacek)

We lived about two miles from school. We walked when it was nice and got a ride in the cold months. Usually it took us a long time to get home from school since we fooled around with the other kids, throwing rocks in the ditches of water, talking, and even playing games. If we were in a hurry to get home, we'd climb the fences and cut through the fields. We had one bike for five of us, so we took turns riding that.
(Marva Rumelhart Ball)

In 1911 when I was six years old, I attended a rural school two miles from my home. On nice days I walked with my older brother, and we joined several other kids along the way. When the weather was rainy or snowy, our dad hitched a team of horses to a lumber wagon or a bobsled and took us. By the time we reached the school, there were at least a dozen kids in the vehicle. Dad was sure he had plenty of horse blankets to cover the noisy kids.

When there was snow on the ground, Dad hitched Old Dan (a pacer) to the cutter, and we drove him to school. My older brother headed Old Dan toward home, and he'd go by himself. One day Old Dan didn't get home when Dad and Mom expected him. They looked up the road and saw him standing beside a telephone pole. For those of you who are unfamiliar with a cutter, the fills are set off center on the cutter so the horse can travel in the track, so you understand why Old Dan was stopped by a telephone pole. Dad tried many times to send Old Dan to school to get us at four o'clock, but Old Dan was a smart horse. When he'd get to the road, he'd turn around and go back to the barn. Since Dad's plan didn't work, it was *he* and Old Dan who came to get us.
(Marjorie Sperry)

We rode to school in a wagon called a "Democrat." My father had built a small shed on the school ground for the horses. I walked to school most of my early days of teaching, through snow, mud, and water. When I started driving, I had many problems driving through snowstorms, rainstorms, etc.
(Eldora Nannestad)

For the first three years, I went to a one-room country school which was located two miles from my home. We had a neighbor girl across the road who was several years older than I, and her father always took her to school with a team and buggy. I got to ride along, but she was sick most of the time so I had to go alone, and two miles seemed like an awfully long way to a six-year-old. In the winter when the weather was bad, I missed a lot of school.

After I finished my schooling, we moved to a farm that had a country school on one corner. During that time the young teacher roomed and boarded at our house. In the spring of the year sometimes the dirt roads were nearly impassable, so I would take the teacher to school on horseback across the fields.
(Harley Oldenborg)

Every pupil, and the teacher, walked to and from school. Buses were non-existent, and very few families owned automobiles. Many of the pupils lived on the south side of the lake (the school was on the north side), and these pupils waited anxiously for the winter freeze so that they could walk across the lake and shorten the distance.
(Ida Posteher Fabyanske)

We recall the fear some children had of a neighbor's dog when they had to go by that farmhouse to and from school. This big dog would seem to hide by the trees, in the tall grass, or in the road ditches. He never barked and you couldn't see him anywhere. Then all at once there he would be, with his nose right down at the children's heels like he was ready to bite. Luckily, he never did. But oh, how he did frighten the children!
(Forrest and Ethelyn McKinley)

I walked to and from school, one mile each way, rain or shine or snow (sometimes knee-deep). It was a fun time to chat with my sisters and brothers while walking to school. I also enjoyed watching the birds and stopping by the pond along the way to watch the frogs

and turtles. I think I enjoy all the beauties of nature so much more having been so close to them in my daily walks to and from school.
(Van Johnson)

Each school district in the southeastern area of South Dakota reached out two and one-half miles in each direction from the schoolhouse — a school every five miles. In those "horse and buggy" days, that was far enough, especially with dirt roads (not even gravel). You went to school on foot, in a buggy, or on horseback. I write of the 1920s.
(Milton S. Johnson)

When I started first grade, my cousin was starting her first year of teaching. Throughout the winter, she lived with us. We were about one and one-half miles from school. Many times in the winter my father took us to school in a horse-drawn cutter, complete with heavy robes and foot warmer, with hot coals in it to keep our feet warm.

Most of the students walked to school, except for one family I recall who lived about three miles from school. They had a horse-drawn cart, in which they rode to school. Many times we would meet them on the corner and get a ride with them.

On our way to school we passed a gravel pit that had water in it. Once this froze over in the fall, we would often stop there and play on our way home. My birthday was November 17, and of course that was one of the days the kids chose to stop and play. I knew if I went down on the ice, I would surely get a "birthday spanking," so I decided I would wait in the cart. It seemed like they were having so much fun and were playing longer than usual, so I finally gave in and went down to play, too. As soon as I got down on the ice, I got my "birthday spanking." They grabbed me by my arms and feet and bounced my bottom on the ice, once for each year, of course.
(Deloris Delage)

In the wintertime nearly all kids, both boys and girls, had their own skis; very few walked to school. We would line the skis up in the schoolhouse, and they would almost fill a whole wall. At recess and noon hour we would run to a little hill just east of Magnuson's driveway, place several sets of skis together, and then sit down on them and slide down the hill. After the path hardened, we sometimes made it all the way to the creek. Then we had to pick up the skis and carry them back to the top of the hill for another try.
(Holger O. Warner)

We got to school by walking a mile or so. The road was a typical gravel road — hot, dusty, muddy, icy, or cold. We were cautioned by Mom not to take rides with anyone, so the day we were offered a ride home by a neighbor, I stuck to my guns and refused. This meant my brothers and sister had to stay with me and continue the long walk home. After we got home, Mom said it was okay to accept a ride if we knew the person. Why hadn't she told me that in the first place?

We would sometimes lay an old purse, with a long string attached, on the road — carefully covering the string with gravel. We'd then take the end of the string and hide in the tall grass until a car came along. When the car stopped, my brother would yank the string hard; then we'd all laugh and run like the dickens!
(Jerrie Steinwall Ahrens)

I walked to school most of the time, but some of the students rode horses. My dad took me to school the first day with a team of mules. We lived one mile west through the field. I knew no one. My teacher gave me a picture of a goose to color. I told my dad I was going to color the feet black, like it had been in the mud. When I looked up, my dad was gone! I cried most of the day.
(Hazel Hubbart Parquet)

I walked about one-half mile to and from school. Sometimes the snow was over knee-high. On the way home one day, I froze all ten fingers. This was very painful when they thawed out. Naturally, all the skin peeled off.
(Signe Haraldson)

We lived about two miles from the schoolhouse and often walked home in nice weather, but my mother or dad usually took us in the morning with the Model T Ford.

One time we had a cart, and we hitched up a horse to take us to school. However, the horse usually got away and ran home ahead, so that didn't work out very well.
(Mary D. Thompson)

One night there was a snowstorm, during which huge snowdrifts accumulated. The hired man took me to school the next morning by sled. When we were about one-half mile from the school, the horses refused to go any farther. I decided to walk the rest of the

19

way, not realizing how deep the snow was. With every step, I'd sink to my knees. I was so sure that I wouldn't make it that I yelled and yelled, hoping someone would hear me. I finally made it to the schoolhouse, but I had frozen my ankles along the way.
(Selma O. Sanvik)

The weather had warmed up and the road was very muddy as I walked the mile to school one March morning. Several young men came along in a farm wagon. Very graciously, they offered me a ride. My boots were muddy, and when I attempted to climb into the wagon, I fell into the mud. The fellows burst into laughter. I stood up and told them they weren't gentlemen and proceeded to give them a lecture on manners. Needless to say, they then jumped out of the wagon and helped me in.
(Edith O. Chaffer)

I walked a mile and a half to school each morning and evening — not too bad a walk if the weather was nice, but this could be an unending distance if it were raining or storming.

I well recall one particular evening when I got a call telling me that there was a bad storm brewing. I hastily put on my warm clothing and began my walk home. Snowflakes were swirling wildly about as I hurried on my way. About halfway home, the storm had become so bad that I could not see the familiar landmarks. I stumbled along blindly, becoming more frightened each minute. Suddenly, I became aware of the field of corn shocks that was at the side of the path I followed across the fields. Now I knew I was on the right path and hurried as fast as possible, nearly losing my breath because of the strong wind. Then the big red barn came into view — perhaps ten feet from me. What a grateful feeling of both surprise and relief overcame me. Yes, I got quite a lecture on the dangers of staying so late at the schoolhouse, and also for not watching the winter weather more closely.
(Margaret Seeger Hedlund)

THE SCHOOL DAY BEGINS

THE SCHOOL DAY BEGINS

The education in a country school was broad and comparatively good. A sense of independence in studying was achieved. "On your honor" meant something if you were to have privileges. You achieved more by being free to move around and get things when needed, not having to wait. All could learn from listening to other classes. If you missed something, you had another chance to pick it up. You had an idea of what the next year would bring. In some ways a rural school teacher was a tutor. A teacher learned to stagger classes and to hold several at one time by doing board work, written guide sheets, and oral work at the same time. There were spelling contests at the school, county, state, and interstate level. It was an honor to be able to take part.

As a teacher, I required at least one book report a period. Schools exchanged books, pupils had library cards in a nearby town, whole schools drove in to a library to get books to keep for a month, and we could get twenty-five books from the traveling library. Pupils recommended books to each other and also exchanged books. They really read quite broadly.
(Arlie M. Klimes)

What I liked so much about country school teaching was that I could arrange things as I liked. It was tutoring, not teaching. Each child went as fast as he could; no moving them along just because it was the next year. Some went faster than others, and the slow ones eventually caught up. I firmly believe that all subjects should be taught in levels, with a test to see if one is ready for the next level.
(Elma Summers)

Children were sent to school whenever the parents decided they were ready. The teacher passed them on according to their ability, so children started anywhere between the ages of four and seven and graduated anywhere between eleven and fifteen.

Having one teacher for all the grades meant that time in class was very limited, so we always had a lot of homework. Consequently, I believe the parents became more involved than those of today. Also, what I consider to have been a decided advantage was that pupils were always able to review what they had studied, since they were

exposed to the same things year after year. If a pupil couldn't master fractions or decimals in his own class, he could always refresh his memory the following year with the next class.
(Ida Posteher Fabyanske)

The education in a one-room school was good, I thought, because you heard what everybody else was studying, so you were pretty smart by the time you went through the eight grades.

I remember when we got a wind-up phonograph and some good records, so we had our own "music appreciation" hour. We had to be able to recognize the piece, giving its name and composer. The same with picture study. We would be expected to know the name of the picture and its artist. We also had penmanship classes, learning to write by the Palmer method.
(Mary D. Thompson)

Most classes were very small, with only one or two in a class. Older children helped the younger ones. Some studied while others recited, and it all seemed to come out right. They learned a lot by just listening.

When I was in the first grade we got a lot of busy work, which was exactly that. The teacher put numbers on our desks with chalk, and we outlined them with corn. At recess time she swept them all into a box. Sewing cards were better because we could take them home.

In the early 1900s we had many newcomers, mostly from Norway or Germany, who came to school to learn English. They were often young men. Sometimes the pupils were nearly as old as the teacher, as the boys had to help at home and only attended in the winter months. Some schools only ran eight months so the boys would be home for spring work.
(Dorothea Thompson)

Every morning we had opening exercises, which consisted of singing, reciting proverbs, or the teacher reading from a library book. We had a library from which we chose books to read. Some were read over and over again.

The size of the classes varied. Sometimes you wouldn't have any pupils in a particular grade. If all classes were filled, you'd maybe have only ten minutes for a class. The most pressure was to try and teach the seventh and eighth graders the right things, as they had to have a mark of 75 on the final exams. Subjects taught were history, geography, language, math, writing, art, and sometimes science.

Friday afternoons were used for art. The girls would sew and the boys did what we called small carpentry work. We also did drawing and painting. We always made a gift for the moms and dads for Christmas.

I think the country schools were a special part of education. The little ones learned from the older ones. No matter what class you were conducting, the rest could listen in.
(Selma O. Sanvik)

Our subjects included reading, writing, the Palmer method of penmanship (which was stressed), spelling (lots of words that we had to learn or else!), arithmetic, history (mostly American), geography, language, and on Friday afternoons we had art. Each grade individually came to the front of the room for recitation. The pupils in the other grades were to study or listen to the class that was being conducted. However, during that time some pupils might throw spitballs or paper airplanes, pass notes to their friends, or maybe even put chalk dust on someone's face or in their hair!
(Elsie S. Fredericksen Williams)

We had reading, penmanship, music, arithmetic, language and grammar, history, geography, physiology, and art. I read most of the books in the library many times and I got many certificates from the county office for library reading.

A county superintendent came a couple times during the year to check supplies, conditions of the school, and the students. We had to take State Board Examinations in the eighth grade. They took turns giving them in the neighboring schools several miles away. We always walked the distance to take the tests. Mom usually made a special lunch for us for the event. I can remember mincemeat pie was a favorite treat, along with some special fruit, which made the long trek more enjoyable.
(Ada Ronnei Pederson)

We always had a so-called monitor each week. The hand bell was rung by one of the students. The day started by pledging allegiance to the flag, and the teacher always read one chapter from one of the classics.

A lot of our work in reading was memorizing, and a lot of it stayed with you through the years. We had to draw maps of all the con-

tinents, put in all the countries, and know the capitals. Each class went to the bench in front for recitation.
(Lucille Siefkes)

Subjects taught were reading, history, geography, civics, language, spelling, arithmetic, and science. We had penmanship once a week and also art. Penmanship papers were sent in to the county superintendent's office and the best ones got certificates. We had Y.C.L. (Young Citizens' League) days once a year and the best art, penmanship papers, and booklets were sent in. We also had spelling contests and the best spellers went on.
(Marva Rumelhart Ball)

The first book I remember learning to read was *The Sunbonnet Babies*. When I began selecting library books to read I remember I liked biographies and autobiographies, and I still do.

I have often felt that my elementary teachers in country school did a very good job teaching the math processes. We practiced and practiced for speed and accuracy in addition, subtraction, multiplication, and division. We worked on spelling, too. Spelldowns were common practice.

To graduate from the eighth grade, students had to pass State Exams. We spent weeks and weeks studying old examination questions. All our grades on report cards, tests, and papers were written in percentages, with 75 as a necessary grade for passing.
(Selma Anderson Hughes)

Friday afternoons were the only times we had music or art. Music included singing from *The Golden Book of Songs* (Old Black Joe, Yankee Doodle, Battle Hymn of the Republic, etc.).

We had a lot of spare time before the teacher called us to the front of the room to recite. I spent much of that time completing a booklet, writing stories out of encyclopedias, and copying jokes out of magazines.
(Margaret Jenkins)

No two children were allowed out of their seats at any one time. The children raised their hand, pointing one finger if they wanted to go to the toilet, two fingers if they wanted to sharpen their pencil, three fingers if they wanted to speak to another pupil, four fingers if they wanted to use the dictionary, and their whole hand if they

wanted to contact the teacher. That way the teacher could look up from a class in progress and know what the child wanted to do, nodding her head if permission was given, and not disturbing the class.
(Ruby Vickers)

The smartest high school students always came from the rural schools. They were especially smart in reading and spelling. Phonics was always an important part of education for all beginners in our school days. Later, when we were teachers, we were all good readers and spellers. Today, in so many grade schools, phonics and other good aids are not taught to beginners, resulting in a generation of such poor readers and spellers.
(Carol Johnston Jeddeloh)

All my eight years of elementary education were in a rural school, and I have never felt that my education was neglected because of it. Since all classes were in one room, younger and older pupils benefited from listening to other classes. Classes were not restricted to the 3 R's. I remember having a man teacher who taught cooking, sewing, manual training, and crafts. I still have a laundry bag that I made in the seventh grade — over seventy years ago.

Country children were shy and sometimes ridiculed by "town kids" when they started high school, but teachers were ready with praise. They said "country kids" were better disciplined, had more respect, and had no trouble keeping up scholastically.
(Mabel Winter)

To graduate from eighth grade you had to take State Board Examinations that were really some humdingers. Some of the answers to those questions I, the teacher, didn't even know!
(Helen C. Williams)

It was customary to have Friday afternoons reserved for such special activities as art and industrial arts. There definitely was a male/female division for such projects, but there was some overlapping. I had a strong interest in art, so these were "red letter days" for me. We "published" a school newspaper, actually one copy only, which was sent home from family to family. I remember doing covers and illustrations for it. I even recall doing a picture of the students around the wiener roast bonfire and trying to dress them up in their usual jackets and sweaters. The wiener roast was a treat for raking the schoolyard.

State Board Examinations were the dread of every eighth grader because the exams had to be passed before getting one's eighth grade certificate. It was possible to take the exams over again, and I think some of the seventh graders tried them also. We had study booklets with sample State Board questions, and we labored over them in preparation for the exams.
(N. Wyelene Fredericksen)

During World War I, schools taught crocheting, knitting, and tatting. Many students knitted squares from wool yarn, khaki-colored, later to be put into blankets for the soldiers.
(Forrest and Ethelyn McKinley)

In addition to the traditional thread of mastery of facts and skills in the subject areas being a "must," emphasis was also placed on developing a pupil's potential for self-discovery. As a result, activities such as science experiments, making graphs, charts, posters, booklets, or other projects to enrich learning were encouraged. These items made up the room displays at completion time and were entered in the Waseca County Fair at the end of the year. Prize money, whether it was $1 or 50^c, was a welcome income for these students. Likewise, it served as an incentive to develop original ideas in the future.
(Hannah Lambert)

The school superintendent came once a year. I remember the teacher getting things cleaned up and giving us more assignments. The superintendent would come and sit by the teacher's desk and stare at us kids all day. We were all afraid of her because of the warnings we got and because she looked so stern.
(Diann Lundeby Wilson)

Eighth grade graduation was a big day. For our final tests we had to go to a town school, and for the graduation we went to a big church about fifteen miles from home. After the eighth grade, most kids stayed and helped on the farm. Many couldn't afford to go to high school.
(Ella Bieberdorf)

School attendance was very important, and striving for perfect attendance was stressed. I still have an Attendance Certificate (part of a book of Friendship Verses) which I received for perfect attendance the entire school year of 1949.
(Norma Hughes Schlichter)

Having taught for thirteen years in the rural schools of Blue Earth County from 1931-1945, I look back and try to evaluate the niche into which the "Little Red Schoolhouse" fit in our society. These were rural communities, and many of the children felt their education was complete after the eighth grade. I know it was impossible to add many frills, but believe me, if capable, they learned the basic 3 R's. I knew each parent and that helped to solve many problems in learning, as well as discipline. I firmly believe that with the closing of our rural schools (small schools), we have lost the last stronghold of our democracy.
(Frances Crook Olson)

I am one of those people who feel we lost something very vital to children's development when we disposed of the rural schools. Now we continually combine/pair schools until the kids will be simply numbers, not individuals. To counteract that "progress," we have to hire child psychologists/counselors so the children can experience a one-on-one relationship.
(Alice L. Soffa)

I, for one, think that we were "sold a false bill of goods" with the big idea to "haul them all into town, have a big school, and you will automatically have better education." We could read and write, spell, and figure when we graduated, and I think we got a good eighth-grade-level education. We were taught the real basics. When the other classes were called forward to recite, the rest of us "listened in," resulting in a lot of "cross-fertilization." When we got to the upper grades, we had been there before. And when you learn spelling at fifteen words a day for several years, you don't misspell many words. And when you learn the multiplication tables with your mother breathing down your neck, and when you memorize Longfellow and Whittier and can reel some of it off fifty years later — well, the "Little Red Schoolhouse" did its job well and was a factor in both education and rural social life. The dismal reports nowadays of being unable to read, write, figure, and spell are quite an indictment of our large educational factories of today. We can't go back; I'm not suggesting it. But we have to get better.
(Milton S. Johnson)

THE "SCHOOLMARM"

THE "SCHOOLMARM"

I began teaching in District 45 in Pope County in September 1923. I had received my first grade teaching certificate from St. Cloud Teachers' College. I taught all the grades from the first to the eighth and I had twenty-one pupils. I stayed with a nearby family during the week and paid out $20 a month for room and board. I learned to like tomatoes while staying there, as I got tomato sauce at every evening meal!

In school I was the janitor as well as the teacher. I swept the room, using a lot of sweeping compound. Two women in the district washed the windows and floor once a month. It was hard to keep the schoolhouse warm, but when it was very cold, I would put into the stove two buckets of hard coal, staying to see that it would burn and keep fire all night. There were lots of ashes to carry out. I was always at the school early in the morning, so I took out the ashes before any pupils arrived at school. The outhouses also gave me lots of work after a snowstorm. There would be drifts to walk through and then if the doors had been blown open by the wind, snow often drifted in.

My salary was different through the years. The lowest I was paid was $50 and the highest was $400 a month. I enjoyed teaching in the rural schools. I taught for twenty-five years and have many happy memories. I was lucky to have had very nice pupils
(Agnes Brenden)

As teacher I was also the school nurse, disciplinarian, psychologist, janitor, arbitrator, and more, besides teaching, and I was only a couple years older than some of the pupils. As a teacher I remember preparing the orders for supplies and hoping the board wouldn't think I was extravagant or lazy if I felt I needed workbooks.
(Alice L. Soffa)

I graduated from high school at Clarkfield, Minnesota, at the age of sixteen. I went on to take another year of really intensive training for teaching in a rural school in the High School Training Department. I graduated in 1924; there were eleven girls in my class. I was not granted a first grade certificate upon graduation, however, because of my age. As soon as my eighteenth birthday rolled around, I was fully accredited.

My first school was near Minneota in Yellow Medicine County. The oldest students were almost as old as I was. I had never attended a rural school, so teaching in one was a whole new ball game for me. I walked back and forth to school on the coldest and snowiest days, often to find that the old stove had gone out overnight. What I knew about stoking a fire you could stick in your eye and you wouldn't feel it! Often you fired only with wood, even overnight.

After teaching three years in Yellow Medicine County, I attended Mankato State Teachers' College, as it was called then, and received a lifetime certificate to teach in town schools. While there I developed an interest in working with the rural department of the college. They would send groups of two, three, or even four at a time out to do their practice teaching for six-week periods. Then you got a new batch. Here I might say that I was getting $70 a month from the school district and an added $10 a month from the college. As I look back, I wonder how I ever did all that work — thirty-five kids in all eight grades — and those practice teachers, some of whom were real "greenhorns." Those were the days! I think of teachers nowadays with their top wages and aides to help with their work, and still they strike for more. Maybe if they'd lived through times like I did, they'd think twice.
(Helen C. Williams)

I started teaching in 1931. During the Depression years teachers were poorly paid. Salaries of $25 and $35 were common. However, I don't remember getting less than $75. (Compare that to what teachers get a month now.) At times there were so many teachers for every job that they underbid each other. Of course the school boards, which were also hard up, would hire the lowest bidder. School boards had a different code of ethics.

After you had a job, getting paid could be a hassle. School boards were short of money, and teachers were often given orders instead of checks. These had to be signed by all three board members. We picked it up from the treasurer, took it to the clerk, and then to the chairman. Often they weren't home and we'd have to go back. No one ever thought of taking it to the teacher. That would make it too easy for her; teachers had to earn their salaries!
(Dorothea Thompson)

I didn't get a chance to teach in a rural school until the Second World War — the 1940s. I graduated from Mankato State and taught social studies and English in junior high school until I was married

in 1920. Then no more teaching until I saw an ad in the *Free Press* — "Rural school teachers needed. Please would any retired teacher come to our assistance and take a school for a few months until the war is over and the regular teachers are back?" Well, I jumped at the chance. The first school I got was the brick school in Butternut and I had eight pupils. I loved it.
(Elma Summers)

My salary the first year I taught (1932) was $70 a month. I paid $14 a month for board and room. A quote from my contract stated, "Miss Anderson agrees to do all janitor work, with the exception of scrubbing the floors and woodwork and the washing of windows." I learned how to get the fire going on Monday mornings and then to fix it at night so there would still be coals to get it going easily the next morning. We had coal for fuel.
(Selma Anderson Hughes)

I had several surprises when I began teaching in a country school, since I had never gone to one or even been in one before I began teaching. Can you imagine that? Surprise Number One — I went to the board and told them I could find no teachers' textbooks. I had no idea that the teacher used the pupils' books! However, the board bought me a whole new set of needed books. How nice! Surprise Number Two — I was used to water fountains at our consolidated school. I soon learned from the children that each morning water was carried in from a pump and put into a so-called water cooler. As far as I'm concerned, it really never kept the water cool. The pupils always took care of the water voluntarily each morning; they were so good about it. Surprise Number Three — no piano! We sang with a phonograph and learned many songs from records. The board bought us a second-hand piano at semester time. And of course — the outside toilet! I always laughed to myself at how many needed to "leave the room" on beautiful days and when it was very, very cold, no one seemed to leave. Strange, huh?
(Clara G. Hagedorn)

I attended Mankato Teachers' College and graduated from the Junior High Department in 1926. At the time of my graduation, teaching positions in Blue Earth County were difficult to obtain, as teachers were holding on to their positions. New graduates were going out into country schools whenever openings could be found,

rather than risk having no position at all. So in September 1926, I found myself in the South Lincoln School, with thirty youngsters from ages six to fourteen, and all eight grades! I'd never had a day of primary or intermediate training, and it was an entirely new world to me. I tried to bring in new ideas and came to enjoy the work. Some tell me that I was their favorite teacher.
(Reba Clark Meixell)

In rural schools we were not only teachers, but janitors and firemen as well. None of us would trade our experiences and memories of the schools. We attempted to keep the school in top condition at all times, fearing the visit of the county superintendent, who would drop in unexpectedly. I think the country schools contributed their part ably in the education system and we can be proud of all of them.
(Clara Anderson)

My sister taught in country schools for over twenty years. I remember the first check she received from teaching. The banker hesitated giving her the money when she wanted to cash it, as he thought she looked too young to be a teacher.
(Mabel Barsness)

The country school teacher started the wood fires each morning and kept the schoolroom clean and in order. At times she got extra help from the pupils. Often they erased and washed the blackboards and had the job of taking the erasers outside and pounding them together to get the chalk dust out. A well-liked teacher probably received a lot of good help!

One teacher planned a nice surprise for her pupils. This was back in the years when the school had a hard-coal heating furnace. When the coals were red hot, the furnace door was opened; then, using a long-handled screen corn popper, the popper was held over the coals, shaking it until all the corn was popped. The students helped, too, and all enjoyed that popcorn treat. This was one fun day that took place on a Friday, after the last recess. Often there were games and other special events which were planned by the teacher for Fridays.
(Forrest and Ethelyn McKinley)

After high school graduation in 1940, I attended Northern State Teachers' College in Aberdeen, South Dakota, for one year, and I received a certificate to teach in a rural school. I taught in the very school where I had been a student for four years. I drove my brothers' Model A Coupe back and forth to school (three and one-half miles one way) and stayed at home with my parents. I paid my brothers a very small amount for the use of the car and gas. I didn't pay my folks anything, but I worked in the house.

My wages the first year (fall of 1941) were $65 a month. I carried the water (for which I received $3 a month) in a large water can. My second and last year of teaching I received $80 a month — quite a raise! The school now had an oil burner, so I didn't have to build fires.

(Mary D. Thompson)

After high school I took a year of Normal Training (as it was called). This entitled me to teach in the rural schools. I taught in several districts. We began the school day at nine o'clock. We had a fifteen-minute recess in the forenoon. Then everyone would peek into his or her lunch bucket for a snack before playtime. At noon we had an hour break. During the winter we sometimes shortened that to half an hour. In the afternoon we had another fifteen-minute recess. If there was anything left in the lunch pail, it was a delightful find. School closed at four o'clock. I always played games with the children at recess time. We were like one happy family.

During the winter it was hard to keep the room warm at times. I had a furnace in one school, but usually it was the big jacket stove. In the evening the fire had to be banked, with the hope that some coals would still be alive in the morning so I wouldn't have to start from scratch. I usually carried matches, as at one school the padlock for the entrance door would freeze, so I would have to thaw it out.

(Selma O. Sanvik)

I vividly remember having to build fires. I had to learn fast. I used corn cobs to start the fire; coal was used for heating. During cold weather in the winter, I learned with good success how to bank the coals with ashes so the fire would remain overnight. Pretty nice to come to a schoolroom with some heat; then I could get the fire going quite easily with the HOT coals. With coal, one must always burn off the gases before closing the drafts and dampers. We had to think of the fire hazards, too, leaving a building unattended for fourteen hours or so.

(Orline Golden Foelschow)

I started teaching after four years of high school, plus one regular term and a summer session at Moorhead Teachers' College. Later I attended many summer sessions at Bemidji and one year at Gustavus. I taught for nineteen years, all in rural schools in Traverse County. There were hardships — like walking to school on a cold Monday morning and finding the room temperature at zero degrees. There were no telephones or indoor toilets. We suffered through the Depression years, as did other folks. One year I taught for $50 a month, and some of that went for books and supplies for the school. I paid $18 a month for board and room.
(Mabel Winter)

One thing that was very apparent when a new teacher came into the school district was the race as to which one of the local boys would get the first date and, hopefully, marry the girl. It's surprising to find how many teachers remained in the community because of this fact. My first experience at the age of eighteen was no exception.

The Palmer Store near District 10 was a gathering place for the local boys during their off hours. Card playing provided them with many hours of fun. There must have been some monetary investment and remuneration, as I found one of the local fellows the frequent winner of a box of chocolates. He would bring this box of chocolates to the school and then offer to give me a ride to my boarding place. In spite of his good intentions, I never dated him.

However, there was a certain Waseca basketball player whom I dated occasionally. He and his friend would come out into the country and pick up my girlfriend, and we'd be back in time for the boys to play the game. One particular afternoon this basketball player called to say he'd pick me up at six-thirty. The Palmer Store was on the same party line as the school. Evidently, there had been some "rubbering" at the store, since the aforementioned "candy bearer" came to the school when it was time to take me home and literally kidnapped me by taking me all the way to Mankato and not bringing me home until eleven o'clock. This caused a few anxious moments for my date, as well as for the boarding house.

Three weeks later, I was met by the sheriff and his deputy as I came to school one morning. It seems that this persistent fellow had sold mortgaged property and had skipped the country. His mother had told the sheriff that he had been seeing the "School Marm" and

was sure I knew where he was. I wasn't even aware that he was missing or gone!
(Hannah Burtness)

My first priority after receiving my teaching certificate was to "get a school," as we said. It meant writing stilted letters of application, stating one's qualifications. I felt ill at ease doing this. We hadn't been taught to think highly of ourselves, but out of necessity I had to do this now. I recall the day I went to call on the three board members, each in his own house. This was my first year. When I drove into the clerk's yard, I met a classmate driving out. I was the third applicant that day. I was hired for the school, a seven-month school, at $75 a month. Was I glad! I had a school! The first week there I wonder if I slept a night through. There was so much to do and I was so nervous.
(Sophie C. Vold Hauge)

School board members were indispensable to a rural teacher because they so unselfishly gave of their time to help with reports, to order supplies or books, set up the school calendar, put up the stage, mow the lawn, fix the furnace, pull the teacher out of a snowbank, or help in other emergencies. The wives were also invaluable in getting the school ready for fall opening by supervising the cleaning and putting up clean curtains, or even making new ones.
(Dorothy Powell)

When I began teaching, I had six weeks of college training and two hours credit from an extension course. I received $80 a month most of the time, once receiving $90 and another time $110 a month.

On the first day of school one year, the wife of one of the school directors was very gracious to me. She told me she had cleaned the school and worked hard at it. She said she didn't disturb the teacher's desk because she thought I'd prefer to clean it. When I opened the desk drawer, out jumped a mouse! The children broke into laughter. Several of the boys gave chase and killed it. The children said that was nothing; all their teachers had mouse trouble. One used to stand on her chair while the boys chased and killed the mice. I laid in a supply of traps and soon had control.

One morning I came to school and saw that a mouse had gotten caught by its tail and was running around the room dragging the trap. I couldn't stand handling mice, so when a boy walked by my school

on his way to catch a ride to high school, I asked him to come in and do away with the mouse. He did so, with a laugh that he tried to hide.
(Edith O. Chaffer)

In one school I had fourteen students — all grades. It was rationing time then, and I had gotten a 1935 Ford from my brother. It was two miles around the road to school, and the parents gave me gas to drive if I'd take their children. I picked up four families — seven children.

I remember well having only two days of school during the month of February and the first two weeks of March one year, as all but two of the pupils had the whooping cough. We didn't have to make up the days, but we had longer assignments.
(Hazel Hubbart Parquet)

Several of the teachers stayed at our home while they were teaching. We really enjoyed having them. Our mother enjoyed cooking and baking, and she made especially good things for the evening meal. She would set the table in the kitchen for the family. The table in the dining room was set for the teacher, and one of us girls took turns eating with her. We really looked forward to our turn.

The teacher's room, I'm sure, was not too warm, but every morning our mother would send one of us upstairs with a pitcher of hot water for washing. There wasn't any running water, hot or cold, or any indoor bathroom facilities in those days on the farm. A white enameled pail, called a slop jar, was used for waste water, and a big white wash bowl and pitcher of water, with towels and soap, were provided in the teacher's room.

The teacher walked to school, and from experience I know the schoolroom was pretty cold when she got there. Usually it was comfortable enough by the time the pupils arrived. Most of the teachers we had came from a distance, so they stayed weekends, too, and they went home only for holidays. We had many enjoyable times with the teachers who stayed in our home.
(Ada Ronnei Pederson)

We would have the teacher over for a meal every once in a while. Some kids would be jealous if they knew the teacher had been to our house for supper. One teacher had her own car, a Model A Coupe, but usually they did not own a car. I remember my first grade teacher

because she had such outstanding blood veins in her hands! Another teacher I had for third and fourth grade was a good teacher and a nice person, but I remember best her chunky beads and how she had a different pair for every dress. I was a good student and I guess I liked all of my teachers because they treated me well.
(Mary D. Thompson)

My grandfather was treasurer of the school board, and I felt extremely important when I was allowed to carry the teacher's monthly salary envelope (sealed, of course) to school. School board members were highly respected, and pupils were instructed by the teacher to be on their best behavior when a board member paid the school a visit.
(Ida Posteher Fabyanske)

My teaching career started in 1934 at the age of nineteen years, after one year of teacher's training. Having attended a rural school for eight years helped immensely. I taught in the rural schools, grade one through grade eight — then later, grade one through grade six — for twenty years. One school I taught in I had only seven students, another had twenty-five, and in one school I had forty some students in all eight grades, with twelve students in grade one. That was a challenge, but very rewarding. During this time I took "off campus" college courses and attended St. Cloud State College during summer sessions and night classes, finally getting my four-year degree. My beginning salary in 1934 was $45 a month for only nine months. The salary gradually increased each year, but not enough for me to be able to take off a year or two to attend college.

Each year we had what was called the "Teachers' Institute." This was held in the court house, and each rural teacher attended. There were workshops led by people from the State Department of Education, where new ideas and innovations were brought to us. Also, ideas were exchanged between teachers. This was very helpful and enjoyable. At one of these I remember writing down all the different jobs a rural teacher had — teacher, mother, nurse, custodian, lawyer, policeman, and counselor. Quite a responsibility!
(Margaret Thompson Cimenski)

For grades one through seven I attended school in town. Then they were going to charge $3 a month tuition for each child, so my dad said we had to go to the country school in our district. The teacher

I had that year was pregnant and not feeling too well, so she let me do a lot of the teaching of the younger children. Of course I thought that was great and it is probably the reason I decided to go to Mankato Teachers' College, as it was called then. I graduated from there with a certificate to teach lower elementary and in rural schools.

One of the boys I had in seventh grade later on married my youngest sister. I was glad to have him in school, as he carried in the wood for the old stove. He also filled the water pail when needed. It is funny people weren't sick more, as we all drank out of the same dipper.

(Viola Burnett Campbell)

As a teacher in a one-room country school, I spent four of the happiest years of my life. I taught in the same school all four years. The average number of pupils was twenty-two, and I had all eight grades inclusive. It was necessary to build the fire after I arrived at the school. I did all the janitor work also. There was no running water or telephone. I was one of the better-paid teachers, as my salary was $110 a month. The year I left, the teacher's salary was dropped to $65 a month. No married teachers were allowed.

(Ruby Vickers)

While attending high school, the thought often came to me that I would like to be a school teacher. In 1918, my dream came true when I graduated from high school and a year of teacher's training. The first school I taught in was in the western part of Pope County. My salary was $70 a month, which to me was indeed a large sum. I paid $18 or $20 for room and board.

The first day of school I did not know exactly what to expect, but I learned fast. When I came to school the first morning, one of the school board members was there to show me around — especially the heating system and how to take out the ashes from the big stove. I quickly learned that there was much more to rural school teaching than just teaching subjects!

Before classes started in the mornings, we always enjoyed singing songs. After study periods of reading, writing, spelling, and phonics, classes were called to the front to recite. Of course we also had spelling bees; how proud the children were when they went to the head of the class. The children were all so lovely, and it was truly a pleasure to work with such fine boys and girls.

(Olive Barsness)

I taught in rural schools from 1917 to 1923. At my first job I earned $60 a month. I taught all eight grades — twenty pupils. A few happenings stand out in my memory: the barn owl that got inside the schoolhouse and perched on our Christmas tree; the nest of newborn baby mice that I found in my desk one morning; the small daughter of a Russian family who spent her first year just "listening," since I knew no Russian and she knew no English; the boy we lost from diphtheria before anyone suspected, and the quarantine that followed; and the horrible black measles I caught the last week of school.

I also remember the time a wagon load of gypsies parked near the school. After morning recess, we discovered that one little first grader was missing. I was beside myself with fear that she'd been kidnapped by the gypsies, but we eventually found her under a table in the basement, crying because someone had hurt her feelings. *(Blanche Lindholm Johnson)*

During my teaching years, I boarded with a family in the district, which was the custom at that time. At each of my boarding homes I paid $15 a month. This does seem cheap, doesn't it? But then one must consider that my salary the first year was $55 a month and I believe the last two years it was $60. These wages were very average or could perhaps even be called "good" for the years of my teaching.

Dad took me to my boarding place on Sunday afternoons and returned for me on Fridays after school. The trip to get me was a big event in the life of my family. Usually Dad was accompanied by my mother, sisters, and brother, so they could enjoy the ride and have a chance to visit. This trip was perhaps the longest one our car made, my school being about fourteen miles south of Glenwood. To reimburse Dad for the time and the wear and tear on the car, I would buy tires when necessary and help out with the gas bills. Also, with a regular paycheck coming in, there were many things I could buy for my family.

During cold weather Dad would go to the schoolhouse with me on Sundays to help split the chunks of wood into kindling or help me pile the larger chunks in neat rows at the side of the entryway. There was a large coal and wood shed in back of the school. I became quite adept at making the fire in the big jacketed stove and also mastered the art of banking the fire before going home in the evening, thereby assuring me of some heat when arriving in the morning. Banking was done by putting a pail of coal carefully over the red hot coals that were burning low in the firebox, and then placing a layer of ashes from the ash pan over the top of the new coal I had just put into the stove. It was most important to make a "breathing hole" in the top of the banked fire or else the fire could smoke or perhaps even explode in one big damaging puff.

Teachers were always invited overnight to each house at least once during the school year. How proud the children were to say, "Teacher came to our house last night."

My three years of being "Schoolmarm" of District 73 have left many pleasant memories in my mind. You might ask, "Would you do it over again?" My answer would be, "I certainly would!"

(Margaret Seeger Hedlund)

THOSE "SYRUP PAIL" LUNCHES

THOSE "SYRUP PAIL" LUNCHES

Lunches were brought from home. Each child had a pail of some sort for his lunch, usually a syrup pail. Some lunches might consist of cold pancakes. Some children I knew had lard on their bread in place of butter. Sometimes there might be a treat. Mothers sent the best they had. There were no hot lunches or milk breaks in those days, although sometimes things might be heated on top of the stove. I can remember baking potatoes in one furnace.
(Dorothea Thompson)

We brought our noon meal in some kind of a pail or lunch box, and it usually consisted of sandwiches (maybe even salmon!), fruit, and a dessert (usually cookies). My mother used to "start" our oranges for us when we were little — by cutting off the stem top, and around the edges she made slits so we could peel off the quarters.

One funny little thing I recall is my friend eating a cookie while she was writing on the board with chalk and getting mixed up and trying to take a bite of the chalk instead of the cookie. We giggled over that.

An innovation was when the mothers decided to have hot lunches during cold weather. Each family took turns serving one day. I recall with embarrassment one family bringing bean soup, and we all got the silly notion that it had worms in it, when what we really saw was the embryo of the bean seed!
(N. Wyelene Fredericksen)

Our lunch buckets were kept in the cloakroom, except in real cold weather, when they were put by the stove so the food would be thawed out by noon.
(Lucille Siefkes)

We got up early in the morning to prepare our lunch for school. That lunch usually consisted of a couple slices of buttered bread, meat of some kind, or maybe some homemade apple butter, and either an apple or an orange. At noon time our lunches were cold, so a kind teacher let us toast our sandwiches in the large heater stove. We sharpened a lath, which teachers used in those days to start the fire when they came to school in the morning, and stuck the sharpened

lath into our sandwiches and held them over the nice red hot coals.
(Elizabeth Juhl)

Our school lunches consisted of sandwiches from home. If we were lucky, we might have cookies or cake, and maybe an apple or an orange. We thought it was a real treat if we had "boughten" bread, which meant we bought it at the store or bakery! Our mother made delicious homemade bread at least three or four times a week, but of course kids like something different once in a while. If we were lucky, we might have a thermos bottle and bring cocoa, but sometimes the teacher made cocoa on top of the heater, too. Lunches were pretty monotonous, but we survived. Some of the kids who were really poor only had lard on their bread! We always had homemade butter because my dad and brothers milked cows, and we had our own milk and cream. Homemade bologna in the winter was also a treat.

When I was teaching, we often would bake potatoes on top of the stove, or one of the mothers might make a rice or bean dish (with surplus commodities), and we'd reheat it on top of the stove.
(Mary D. Thompson)

Lunch time was like a family time in the rural school. Each student brought his lunch in a pail of some sort. When I was a student, we used syrup pails and envied those who had "real" lunch boxes.

When I taught, most of the students had lunch boxes, except some of the boys who didn't want to be bothered and brought theirs in sacks. We all sat at our desks and ate together. This was a learning time, too, as we discussed good manners, etc. I asked them to sit quietly at least ten minutes. Then those who were finished were dismissed for play.
(Margaret Thompson Cimenski)

Lunches were provided in various ways. Pails were used as containers. There was often bartering of food. One girl had only a pancake at times. Jars of food were placed in warm water on top of the stove. In very cold weather mothers took turns bringing hot food, enough for all. One could bake a potato in the ashes.
(Arlie M. Klimes)

We always carried a cold lunch. A popular menu was a peanut butter and jelly sandwich, with a piece of fruit and some cookies

or a bar for dessert. When the weather was warm, we could go out-side to eat our lunch. After we finished our lunch, we usually had time for a short softball game before we had to go in for classes again.
(Van Johnson)

There was no hot lunch program available when I went to school. We carried our lunches from home, probably something like this: homemade bread, mayonnaise, leftover roast beef or egg salad, cheese on Fridays, maybe head cheese, a home-canned pickle, an orange or banana or apple, and once in a while, a powdered sugar doughnut. Now those doughnuts were good "trading" material!

In the colder weather the older girls in the room helped the teacher make hot chocolate for lunch time. I remember my sister always helped. Sometimes I helped pass out the crockery — white farmer coffee cups. Oh, the smell of that chocolate still sweetens the memory! I think there might have been a charge of three cents.

Our lunches were wrapped in newspaper (food was individually wrapped in wax paper) and then tied with string. The smell of food and newspaper is quite delightful yet. Special times of the year we were given free samples of "mentholatum" in a very small, flat tin (it smelled so healthy), and a talk on germs. The pictures were interesting; you didn't get to see germs very often!
(Jerrie Steinwall Ahrens)

We would bring our lunch in a half-gallon syrup pail. We had sandwiches, sometimes a hard-boiled egg, and some cookies or cake. A piece of pie was a real treat. We had plenty of apples from our large orchard, so we had fruit the year round. An orange or a banana was a special treat.
(Ada Ronnei Pederson)

I remember heating a jar of food in a shallow pan of water for noon lunch, or baking a potato on the ledge inside the furnace. Bump the potato and the hot lunch burned to a crisp! We carved our initials on the potato so we got our own.
(Alice L. Soffa)

All the children carried their lunches from home in a tin Karo syrup pail. If more than one child from a family was going to school, they used the gallon size. Lunch was basically a syrup or jelly sandwich. We seldom had meat sandwiches and very little fruit,

mostly at Christmas time. We seldom had dessert unless we had celebrated a birthday or other special event. No one carried milk. We drank water which was pumped from outdoors and then put into a fountain in the school entryway.
(Lucina E. Valento)

Regarding the noon lunches, the teacher lived close enough so that she could go home, as did a number of the pupils. Most of us, however, brought our lunches from home, wrapped in yesterday's newspaper and tied with grocery string. Lunch bags were not yet available, and no one would have considered "buying" a paper bag to be used once and thrown away. We seldom had anything to drink with our lunches, as thermos bottles were fairly new and "too expensive" for kids.

There was no behavior problem during the teacher's noon-hour absence, since she always appointed a "monitor" who was instructed to write down the names of pupils who misbehaved. The usual punishment was to write the multiplication tables, either on the blackboard or on paper, during the following recess period. Needless to say, by the time we all got out of the eighth grade we were very good at multiplication!
(Ida Posteher Fabyanske)

The years when there was a Mothers' Club that provided noon lunches were special. Each mother would take a turn bringing hot lunch for everyone in the school. We all eagerly waited to see what was going to be brought each day.
(Norma Hughes Schlichter)

IT'S RECESS TIME

IT'S RECESS TIME

(There are several variations in spelling and word structure for some of the games listed in this chapter. For consistency, I have chosen the most common usage.)

Funny, I never remember hearing anyone say, "There's nothing to do" at playtime in the little school on the prairie, even though there was no fancy playground equipment (slides, jungle gyms, or merry-go-rounds); only a pair of sturdy hand-built swings. We enjoyed them and we certainly learned to share. But we didn't always swing. Sometimes in the spring one of the boys would try a little baseball, but with an enrollment of never more than fourteen children, and of course some of them first and second graders, this was never terribly successful. We played "Hide and Seek" sometimes, too, but with a choice of only four places to hide — behind the schoolhouse, the barn, or the "boys," or "girls" — this often got dull in a hurry.

There were, of course, games familiar to children growing up everywhere — "Pump Pump Pullaway," "Tag," "Statue," "Poison Tag," and "Duck Duck Gray Duck." One of our favorites was "Anti Over." We divided into two teams and one went on each side of the schoolhouse. One team would throw the ball and yell "Anti Over." If it didn't go over, you had to yell "Pig's Tail" and try again. If it went over and lit on the ground, their team had to try throwing it over. If someone caught it, they could come dashing around to the other side. Anyone from the opposite team whom they could touch with the ball had to join their team. The game ended when one team had all the players or when the bell rang. Another favorite was "Cops and Robbers," where everyone dashed wildly around the playground either chasing or being chased. If you were caught, you were locked in the woodshed, but if the jailer forgot to say "Tick-tock-double-lock" when you were shut in, then it was perfectly legal for you to escape.
(Mae F. Hardin)

The boys would run outdoors at noon hour and recess yelling, "Batter up, pitcher, catcher, first baseman," telling what position they would play in a game of "work-up." Softball was a game everyone played and became very skilled at.

Other games were "Hide and Seek," "Tin Can" (a version of "Hide and Seek"), "Anti Over" (throwing a ball over the school, with the other side trying to catch the ball before it bounded), "Last Couple Out," "Prisoners' Base," "Pump Pump Pullaway," "Lemonade," and "Fox and Goose" (in the snow). The games required almost no equipment or teacher planning.
(Margaret Jenkins)

Recess was spent with everybody playing together — maybe "Softball," "Captain May I?," "Hide and Seek," or "Tag." Some days we just played on the swings. Once in a while we'd sneak down to a bridge (about one-fourth mile away) where there was a stream, and we'd pretend we wouldn't hear the bell.

In the winter when it was cold, we would play games inside or in the basement. We also played on an ice pond and had snowball fights across the road. Each side had a ditch, and if you hit someone on the other side, they had to come to your ditch. The object was to get everyone on one side.
(Marva Rumelhart Ball)

When it was too cold to play outside in the winter, we would play cards (whist) at recess. Other recess activities were circle games, "Hide and Seek," "Pump Pump Pullaway," and "Anti Over," which was played over the shed in back of the school. The shed was there to house the horses that were sometimes ridden to school by some of the students.
(Deloris Delage)

Our school had a hill behind the barn where we could slide on our sleds in the winter. There was a slough at the bottom of the hill which froze over and made a nice long ride on the sled. During nice weather we played other outdoor games, such as "Captain May I?," "Pump Pump Pullaway," "Baseball," "Hopscotch," "Fox and Goose" (a game played in the snow, with paths in a circle and dissecting lines), and many other games. We also had a teeter-totter, swings, a slide and a merry-go-round, so we didn't lack for things to do.

Of course in the spring we played marbles, too. A beautiful glass marble was hard to come by, and most of our marbles were the smaller clay ones, known as "commies" (for common, I suppose). Sometimes you might be lucky and have a steel one.
(Mary D. Thompson)

At recess time we played jacks, marbles, jump rope, and ball. My brother was good at marbles; he had a lot of them. Some were called "cat eyes," "aggies," "steelies," and of course his "shooter." Mom would make little leather pouches to carry them in. Jump ropes were clotheslines, and some were real long. There was a girl at each end, and you had to be good to play with those older girls. Most of the time you did your jumping individually, but remember, not too much or the shoes might give out!

Also, there was a stream nearby, and we could pick spring flowers or clover and make wreaths and crowns for each other, or hold dandelions under each other's chin to see if you liked butter. If there's a yellow reflection on the underside of your chin, you do like butter.
(Jerrie Steinwall Ahrens)

We had a skating rink about one-fourth mile from the schoolhouse. At noon hour we could run there and do a little sliding around, as very few of us had skates. My brother and I usually walked home across the frozen pond, but we walked across it one too many times. CRACK! CRACK! And we were both in the cold water and ice. We walked home, about a mile, as fast as possible and put dry, warm clothes on. Surprisingly, neither of us even got a cold after that encounter.

After the frost went out of the ground in the spring, the big boys got us to help drown out gophers at recess and noon hour. The boys got old pails out of the woodshed. Some of us had to pump the water, others carried the pails of water to pour down the gopher hole, and the big boys stood there with sticks to kill the gopher when it came out.
(Orline Golden Foelschow)

One activity we had was chasing gophers. These nasty little rodents were very destructive to crops, and multiplied so rapidly that they were more than a nuisance. It didn't matter what game we were playing; if someone spied a gopher, it took immediate priority over any other activity. Away we all flew after it as fast as our legs could carry us. Since they had holes all over where they could pop out of sight almost at will, we were never successful in catching one, but we really tried.
(Mae F. Hardin)

We all played ball in a pasture across the road from the schoolhouse. Girls, as well as boys, played with a hard baseball, as

we all had to play together to have enough for teams. There was a place in that same pasture where an ice pond formed, and we used to skate there. We had clamp-on skates which we fastened directly to our hightop shoes. Warm days developed "rubber ice," which was much fun and not dangerous because the water was very shallow. However, it was very wet, so we had to dry out by the old heater. The gravel pit was to the east, and that provided a very steep place for sliding. It was really very dangerous, so the more daring were the ones who used it most often.
(N. Wyelene Fredericksen)

Toward spring we would have a few thawing days. The potholes in the neighboring fields would fill and then freeze, so for a little while we could go sliding on the ice. Few of us could afford skates, but that didn't stop our fun. This sport sooner or later almost always ended in the same way. Because we loved to slide on the ice, we would try to stretch the season just one day too long, and someone would go through the thin ice. The potholes, for the most part, weren't too deep, so no one was in grave danger. However, whoever it was — sometimes several — got a really icy bath.
(Mae F. Hardin)

We played several games at school. Outdoors we played ball games, "Hide and Seek," "Tag," "Anti Over," and "Pump Pump Pullaway." Inside we played "Fruit Basket Upset," "Guessing Games," "Hide the Thimble," and in the hall we played "Pussy Wants a Corner," "Blind Man's Bluff," and "Drop the Handkerchief." We really had a lot of fun.
(Ada Ronnei Pederson)

Every winter we had our hopscotch tournaments. We drew the hopscotch grids on the floor with chalk. There was only room, by squeezing, for two grids between the seats, so there was one for the big kids and one for the little ones. The competition was really heated. I wonder if any of my contemporaries, sitting tense before a TV during the "Super Bowl," can remember being *just* as excited watching to see whether their favorite player tossed his leather mitten in the right square, or willing him *not* to step on any lines.

Another game we played a lot was "Skip." "It" skipped around the room and tapped someone on the head. This person got up and tried to catch "it" before he reached a circle drawn with chalk on

the floor at the front of the room. If he caught him, he could sit down again. If he didn't, he was "it." The trick, of course, was to *skip*, not run. If you ran, you forfeited, and when you're in a hurry, it isn't always easy to remember to skip, not run. We sometimes played this to help kids thaw out when they came to school in the morning.
(Mae F. Hardin)

Playground equipment in early times was very simple. Our baseball bats often were barrel staves or other discarded boards or sticks. The balls, too, were made at home. Old stockings and sweaters were ripped or cut up and the yarn wound into a solid ball. This was covered with leather from an old boot which had been cut, soaked, and stretched. These balls bounced very well.
(Ruth V. Esping)

Popular recess games were "Run Sheep Run," "Red Rover," "Pump Pump Pullaway," "Duck on a Rock," "Anti Over," "Here Comes the Duke A'Roaming," etc. Weather permitting, there was always a kittenball game in progress.

During the winter months many of the pupils brought sleds to school. This served several purposes — the small children were allowed to ride if big brother or sister was willing to pull; they carried books and lunches; and they were used on the hills during recess time and the noon hour.
(Ida Posteher Fabyanske)

Children (and the teacher) looked forward to recess and noon hour. Many were the games we played. There were many variations of "Tag," "Pump Pump Pullaway," and of course, ball. I was usually chosen last for ball games because I couldn't hit the broad side of a barn!

In winter if we had a creek or a hill nearby, we went skating or sliding, often combining recess and noon hour to have a longer playtime. In the spring we drowned out gophers. On rainy days we played blackboard games or moved back the seats and played circle games. We often had to improvise for play equipment. New things were hard to get, especially if the school board thought it was all "darn foolishment," so the teacher often used her own money to buy bats and balls. One board member thought that we could make our balls and use sticks for bats.
(Dorothea Thompson)

One day some boys brought a one-horse cutter sleigh to school. The box was gone — just the runners with a platform was left. They could sit on the platform and steer it when out sliding. During recess, the teacher (a man) said he could "stand up" and ride down the hill with the boys. The bigger boys sat on the platform, with their feet down so they could steer it. The road had a curve, with trees across the road. They would turn up the road to the left and then would continue to the end of their regular run. This time, however, the boys turned the cutter into the trees and jumped off, leaving the teacher sailing on through the air and into the trees. The teacher never said a harsh word to any of them, but he never rode the cutter with them again either!
(Forrest and Ethelyn McKinley)

One always sees lovely pictures of children building snowmen with funny hats and carrot noses, but there was something about the powdery wind-blown snow in North Dakota which just wouldn't pack right, so we never made snowmen in the winter. On the rare winter days when it was decent to go out, we had to play something active to keep warm. Sometimes it was just "Tag," or if there was a fresh snowfall, we would make a big "pie" in the snow. When the drifts got high, some would bring sleds and slide down their steep sides. These were the only "hills" we had in that flat country.

Of course, much of the time it was just too blue cold to play outside. Anyone who had walked over a mile to school, and maybe frozen a nose or cheek, wasn't all that eager to go out at noon, since they faced the same trip home. And recess was just too short anyway to get all bundled up with all the scarves, mittens, boots, etc., and then take them all off again. Besides, they might not be dried out from when you came in the morning. So when it was bitter cold we stayed in, which limited our activity, to say the least. I'm sure on those days the teacher thought she had a lot more than fourteen pupils!
(Mae F. Hardin)

PROGRAMS, SOCIALS, AND OTHER DIVERSIONS

PROGRAMS, SOCIALS & OTHER DIVERSIONS

A Christmas program was a MUST. We started practicing right after Thanksgiving. We'd hand out the parts to be memorized before Thanksgiving vacation. It was indeed fun to get ready for the "big night." We had to provide a stage, using sheets as curtains. One neighbor would bring a gas lantern for light. Then the last day planks were brought in for extra seating. The fathers were good helpers. The parents brought the lunch and plenty of coffee. When the program and lunch were over, the desks were pushed to the side and the planks were removed. Then, young and old played games and everyone enjoyed themselves.
(Selma O. Sanvik)

The Christmas program was the highlight of the year, rivaled only in importance by the annual school picnic or the visit of the county superintendent. The country school programs were exciting times, both for the child and the parents. Each child always gave a recitation or had a part in a play involving several students. The front of the room was closed off from the admiring audience by an old, much-mended, gray curtain, which was strung by strong wire.

After the program, lunch of hearty meat sandwiches and large pieces of cake was served by the mothers. A bushel basket full of tin cups would be borrowed from an auctioneer for the big celebration at school, and coffee was brought in large gray enamel coffee pots by wives of school board members. The balance of the evening was spent playing games or dancing reels. This part of the evening was much enjoyed by older students and visitors.
(Margaret Seeger Hedlund)

At Christmas you were expected to put on a program for parents and the community. We strung up a curtain across the front of the room, and behind it we tried to have order out of chaos, with all the children, properties, and everything back there. Usually it turned out reasonably well. I always hated all the time it took to practice for those programs because we lost good school time. But it was expected, and often a teacher was judged by the programs she produced.
(Helen C. Williams)

There was always a Christmas program at school put on by the teacher and pupils and attended by nearly everyone. Some programs were given in the afternoon. If the programs were given at night, the families would bring their lanterns and lamps to light up the school building. Along with the program, there was always a lunch. Then we got back into the horse-drawn bobsleigh and headed for home, listening to the ringing of the sleigh bells.
(Forrest and Ethelyn McKinley)

During the Christmas season we spent much of our time practicing for our annual Christmas program. We spent hours cutting out red and green wreaths to use to decorate all the windows. This was always such a happy time. Everyone was in the holiday spirit, and we got to know all of our fellow students so well during this time. All of the students took part in decorating the Christmas tree, which was always placed at the side of the stage, along with a manger scene.

At the end of the program, we had a potluck lunch, which included sandwiches and cake. Sometimes we had a basket social. It was always fun to see who bought our baskets.
(Van Johnson)

I remember practicing for our Christmas program from Thanksgiving on. On the night of the performance, the sight of the lighted schoolhouse caused flutters in my stomach. It was always a thrill getting a box of three pencils with my name on them from the teacher.
(Alice L. Soffa)

Christmas programs were big events. I always had a piano or an organ. In one of my last schools, I taught piano and accordian at noon. I had an eight-piece accordian band, which made programs easy. At the end of one school year, I was given a TV table and lamp at the picnic as thanks for the music lessons.
(Emily Sedlacek)

Christmas programs were always necessary, and we had to get all the children to participate. We had no musical instruments the first years, so the singing was not always kept in tune! Later, we got a phonograph, which helped a lot.
(Signe Haraldson)

Christmas programs were a necessity. They were fun to have, with the makeshift curtains (sheets strung on a wire). My sister (also a teacher) and I bought a record player for the music. I had my program first. The record player was stolen before her program, so I had to sing behind the curtain to help her pupils out!
(Eldora Nannestad)

School holidays were listed on the contract, as was the need to have Christmas programs. There were corn picking and seeding vacations, so we really managed only eight months of school.

For the Christmas program, a stage was set up with blocks, and planks were laid across them. Some schools had old curtains. If not, sheets were used. They sagged, wires broke, and down came the curtains! A placard with instructions was fastened with rope, so all the pupils had to do was walk on, follow the directions, and walk off. Children drew names and gifts were exchanged. Teachers gave a gift to each child and received one in return. Apples, which were furnished by the school board, were passed out to the audience. Teachers filled the children's sacks with goodies.
(Arlie M. Klimes)

We enjoyed getting ready for programs for our parents. There were songs, recitations, and dialogues. We would practice and practice. Sometimes my brother, two sisters, and I could go through the whole program at home because we had learned everyone's part. Sometimes some of us were asked to put on a dialogue at a Farm Bureau meeting.

We always had a Christmas program for our parents. We had a big Christmas tree, on which we put real candles. We lit the candles on the night of our program when the schoolroom was packed with people. As I remember those Christmas trees, I still shake my head and wonder how we dared to do such a thing. We were so lucky.
(Selma Anderson Hughes)

Christmas programs were big events for the whole neighborhood. The teacher would hang up sheets on wire for a curtain. We were all so excited. Of course there was no electricity, so lamps and lanterns had to be brought from the homes for this occasion. I especially remember one time when I was an angel and my wings kept falling off. I almost missed my cue for my part in the program!

We also had pie socials sometimes, where the men would bid on the ladies' pies. Entertainment was cheap in those days, and more

things were done on the local level — such as card parties and even dances in the farmhomes.
(Mary D. Thompson)

In December we worked hard getting a Christmas program together that we could present to the parents. I always enjoyed that when I was a child attending the country school. The school board erected a stage in the front of the building.

After the program, there was a box lunch auction. The women of the district decorated a shoe box which contained lunch for two people. The men were good bidders and wanted to buy their spouse's box. If anyone knew which box was the teacher's, the bidding would usually go high, since the bachelors always wanted to get the teacher's box.
(Agnes Brenden)

Everyone always had a part in the Christmas program. My dad was Santa Claus, and my mother made him a suit. Kids' parents brought quantities of food for lunch after the program. My dad made coffee in a copper-bottomed wash boiler! Later, one of the mothers fiddled and my dad called square dance routines.
(Ruth Aleda Johansen)

School holidays were memorable, as in the fall around Halloween or Thanksgiving, we would put on a program for the neighborhood, with singing, plays, pageants, recitations, etc. Following the program, the ladies' baskets, which had been decorated and filled with lunch, would be auctioned off to the highest bidder; then they ate the lunch together. This was great fun and exciting, especially if there were unmarried ladies in the group. Sometimes the bidding would really be competitive for these baskets. The money from these auctions would then be used to buy Christmas gifts for the school children at Christmas time. The teacher bought these gifts, sometimes with the help of the parents. Some of the money was used to buy Christmas candy and peanuts, and also a box of apples. The candy and peanuts were then put in individual sacks and each child received one. The apples were passed out to everyone.

The Christmas program was quite an event. The real "Christmas Story" was always given as a pageant, along with much singing, other plays, and recitations. Someone always came in dressed as Santa Claus and distributed the gifts.
(Margaret Thompson Cimenski)

Any little programs given by the children were looked forward to by the whole community. Box socials were a way to make a little extra money, which was usually used for books, playground equipment, and other supplies. A program was given, and then the boxes were auctioned off. Each lady or girl packed a box with lunch for two, each one trying to outdo the others. Usually the boxes contained sandwiches, fried chicken, cake, cookies, and fruit. Then she decorated the box, trying to keep her design a secret, and hoping a certain person would get it. The men and boys bought the boxes and then ate with the owner.
(Dorothea Thompson)

A big event in rural schools used to be the basket socials. People came from miles around. Ladies decorated baskets and packed a lunch for two in them. The baskets were then auctioned off to the highest bidder. Usually they went for a couple dollars or less. Once in a while, someone found out whose basket was up for sale and, just for meanness, would run the price up, so the boyfriend might pay up to $10 or more. The money was usually used to buy library books.

People would come in bobsleds, with ten or more people in them. They'd tip the sled over into snowdrifts on the way, just for fun. They played "Four in the Board," "Gustav Skaal" (Norwegian), and many other games before the baskets were sold.
(Helen C. Williams)

As a means of getting some extra equipment for the school, we would have some way of raising money. One year, instead of the ordinary basket social, the ladies and girls brought unusually decorated hats. It was great fun seeing the men and boys bidding on their favorite hats. The rule of the evening was that each owner must wear his hat to get to eat the very delicious lunch the ladies and girls had brought.

At this event the children usually gave a short program. This particular year, the men agreed to entertain the group. Their skit happened to be their impression of the local ladies' bunco club. It was hilarious to see them all dressed as ladies and hear their conversation, which centered on recipes, housework, bits of gossip, and their operations. The evening was a great success and the children thoroughly enjoyed it. With the money earned, the children decided on some new balls and bats, a soccer ball, and games that could be played indoors in cold weather or on rainy days.
(Magdalene Waite)

Something that was done in those days in country school was to have a "Home Talent Play." People from the community were the actors and I, as teacher, was usually the director. Often we put the play on in other communities once it was whipped into shape. That was really fun. You learned a whole different side to people that you didn't know they had.
(Helen C. Williams)

For special fun there were sleigh rides and picnics for the "young people," all of which the teacher was obligated to attend. One time in the fall, all the neighborhood young people went to the woods about two and one-half miles away to gather walnuts and to have a wiener roast. Picnics and wild flower gathering were also sources of amusement.
(Reba Clark Meixell)

A big event in the rural school I attended was "Play Day," a county-wide gathering of school children. The first part of the day was given over to music and "declamation" contests. For weeks before the big event, we'd practice. I always was chosen to speak a "piece." This meant memorizing a story or poem and delivering it with impressive gestures and voice inflections. How nervous I would be! There would always be at least three trips to the bathroom in the hour before it was my time to be "on." Afternoons were given over to track and field contests. Because I was not much of an athlete, my afternoons were free to roam through the stores uptown, admiring the trinkets in the dime stores and eating ice cream cones.
(Pat Hanson)

The last day of school always was the picnic for the entire family. This was usually held in a farmer's pasture, not too far from school. After we'd eaten all the food which had been brought, the softball game was an important event. Others then wandered along the creek.
(Margaret Jenkins)

School picnics at the end of the school year were of special importance. It was about this time of the year that our mothers would let us roll down our socks after a long, cold winter of wearing long underwear and long socks. We felt FREE! I can remember watching other schools in the park that had a big ten-gallon container of vanilla ice cream as a special treat, but we didn't have any. I guess

66

our school board thought it would cost too much money. How we longed for one of those ice cream cones! I'm sure in the later years we maybe had some, but I especially remember the picnics when we didn't have any.
(Mary D. Thompson)

A big spring event in our rural school was the all-school picnic. At nine o'clock in the morning on the last day of school, several carloads of students (our entire school) would go to a nearby state park. It was a glorious day — not too organized! Several tables would be put together and that would become our headquarters. We could run and play. By noon, parents had arrived with food, and a potluck dinner would be held. Dessert would be ice cream — a real treat for kids who lived in a town or on farms that had no electricity — and so no refrigeration. The ice cream had been ordered from the Bridgeman-Russell Company in Grand Forks. It would be brought to our little town by truck, carefully packed in dry ice. It was always my dad's job to wait for the ice cream and then bring it out to the picnic. One year the truck failed to show — what a disappointment! An hour after eating, we would be permitted to go swimming in the river.

Another annual event in the spring was "Clean-up Day." We'd all bring our rakes from home and spend the afternoon raking the schoolyard, cleaning away the winter debris. What treasures were to be found!
(Pat Hanson)

In the spring of the year, we had "Clean-up Day." After raking and starting the bonfires, I furnished all the ingredients for a wiener roast. What fun!

Then on May 1, I hung a "May Basket," filled with goodies, on each desk. The pupils were allowed to eat out of it all day long. One little girl came to me at recess time to see if she could remove her gum. She said, "My jaws are just so tired." Needless to say, I never had any problems with the pupils eating candy or chewing gum in all the rest of the days.
(Frances Crook Olson)

I remember the school picnic at the end of the term, with all those wonderful games of baseball, tug-of-war, gunny sack races, wheel-barrow races (one unlucky kid got to be the wheelbarrow), relay races,

and — prizes! And, of course, food — lots and lots of home cooking. Ladies would pile it high on the tables. I remember taking some corn. It looked so beautiful in the dish, all gold and shiny, but yuk, it was so salty! But we had a good time. It was time to take our shoes off for the summer.
(Jerrie Steinwall Ahrens)

The picnics at the end of the school year were generally held in the woods next to the schoolyard. There would be potato salad, sandwiches, beans, cake, cookies, and lemonade; and the inevitable ants, flies, and mosquitoes (they didn't know of any sprays in those days). And so it was that we said "good-bye" to our teacher and friends until the fall, when in September the term started again.
(Lauretta Cords)

All social life — Christmas programs, social picnics, school plays, community clubs — revolved around the schoolhouse as the one meeting place available. When the country school went, much of the rural social life disintegrated. Its common center, the school, was no more.
(Milton S. Johnson)

FROM SKUNKS
TO SNOWSTORMS

FROM SKUNKS TO SNOWSTORMS

Nature believes in making use of any space available. In 1928, the space under the school seemed a good home for a family of skunks. All went fairly well, with just a slight disagreeable odor at times, until some woodchucks moved in, and ownership of the space was challenged with a fight. We all cleared out of the school in a hurry and rushed home, only to be ordered to leave our clothes and everything else that had been in the school outside. Help had to be called in to gas the animals and deodorize the place, an ordeal which was not perfectly satisfactory.
(Ruth V. Esping)

One dark morning while I was putting lessons on the blackboard at the front of the room, I heard footsteps pacing back and forth in the basement. I was alone and thought perhaps I was imagining things, but the pacing continued. With no telephone or car, I had no way to get help, so I stayed in the room, wondering who or what would open the door and walk in. When the door finally did open, luckily it was a school board member with his children. I told them about the mystery in the basement, and the dad went down to investigate. When he returned, he told us that there was a large skunk in the storeroom trying to get out. He went to get the other two school board members, and when they returned, they used a poisonous spray to kill the animal. They brought it up by the tail and displayed it to us in the schoolroom. Then they went to town to claim the $6 bounty. The skunk had done no damage in the basement, but it always remained a mystery how it had gotten in there.
(Kathleen Rietforts)

I came to the Maker School about 1929, facing a terrific discipline problem. There were five or six "big boys" who were really ruling the roost. The room was so full that the ringleader had to sit on a folding chair behind the last desk in the row. With all those grades, my class time was limited, so I had told the pupils not to ask any questions while I was teaching a class; I'd answer all questions between classes. Almost the first day this fellow raised his hand, and when I didn't come at once from class, he shoved his chair clear back to the wall and sat there defying me. I knew I must

do something drastic or be driven out as the teacher before me. So I walked back to him, tipped him back in his chair to the floor, and got my knee on his chest. Then I said, "Now will you do what I want you to, *when* I want you to?" In a very frightened voice he answered, "Yes." Then I told him to get up, get his dinner bucket, and get out of there. I didn't want to look at him any more that day. He left, but he didn't go home. He stayed in a nearby gravel pit until school was out. He never told anybody at home either, but I did. I heard reverberations of, "I guess that new teacher *means* what she says." I never had any more discipline problems all the years I taught there.
(Helen C. Williams)

Teaching in the early 1900s and during the war and Depression years, as my sister did, brought about some interesting and exciting happenings. My sister told of entering her school one morning and finding it warm. A hobo had slept there and kept the fire going. Gypsies were a common sight, sometimes scary, as most of the children had been told that they stole little ones.
(Dorothea Thompson)

I shall not forget an experience from which I learned a valuable lesson. It happened on a windy, late fall day when I discovered, upon leaving for the day, that I was locked in the schoolhouse. Since there was no telephone or lights in the building, I knew my only way out would have to be through a window. Luckily, they weren't double windows, so at least I could open one. The drop to the ground was too far without something to step on. The only loose objects were six orange-crate chairs for little folks, so I capitalized on using them. The first four fell over as they were dropped, but the fifth one stayed upright. Three times I was about out when I'd hear a car coming, so I'd crawl back in, lest I would be seen. Finally, it quieted down on the road and I made a safe landing, picked up the chairs, and found out why I was locked in. The metal bar had fallen over the padlock staple when the door was slammed shut. From then on I supervised every dismissal of the pupils.
(Hannah Lambert)

In the spring of the year, the creek that was between our farm and the schoolhouse always went out of its banks and made a new path (not under the bridge). When it appeared to be a bit hazardous,

my brother went that far with me in the morning and drove the car across, so that we made it safely. But one afternoon the water got higher and higher and was flowing much more swiftly. He called the neighbors to catch me and tell me to go another way (several miles farther), but because of a snowstorm that afternoon, the neighbors didn't see me come. I approached the watery roadway with caution, but decided to try it anyway. The whole front end of the Model A fell into the washout on the road, and I had to crawl out in ice water up to my hips! Luckily, there were neighbors just a few yards away, and an old German lady found me dry clothes. Then we called my folks, and my dad and brother came after me. But the car had to stay there overnight, and the next day it was completely frozen in. It didn't hurt the motor, but it was not an easy task to get it out and running again. It is a miracle my brother let me keep on driving his car after that episode!
(Mary D. Thompson)

One day I heard a loud bellowing noise, and for some reason I thought the boys were teasing a bull across the road. When I went out to stop them, I discovered that it was the bull himself pawing the ground and trying to get at the children. I called the children in, and in a few minutes the bull tore down three fence posts and brought his harem onto the playground. It was after five o'clock before it was safe to send the children home, as by then the cows went to the barn. In those days no parents rushed to see where their children were. They just assumed they would be home sometime.
(Dorothea Thompson)

One morning in May, the children came to school as usual. There seemed to be an air of expectancy as mischievous eyes watched me during the opening morning exercises. Then out of the desks came noisy sacks. Down the aisles rolled all kinds of canned fruits, vegetables, and glass jars of jelly and pickles. For once, I couldn't say anything, as I didn't understand what was going on. Then one little girl gave me a pretty card with all the children's names on it. She explained that they were having a food shower for me as a going-away surprise. I appreciated the food and the thought that went into planning it, and the surprise became another nice memory of teaching in days gone by.
(Kathleen Rietforts)

One day, before I was old enough to go to school, a teacher who stayed at our place offered to take me along to school. It was a very cold, snappy winter's day, so someone took us to school in a bob-sled pulled by a team of horses. When we got to school, the teacher had to start a fire in the big old pot-bellied stove that stood in the back of the room. As soon as she had the fire going good, the children started to arrive and crowded around the stove to get warm. The teacher, thinking my feet might be cold, sat me in a chair next to the stove and put my feet up against its side. She was getting ready for school to start, when someone yelled, "Lauretta's feet are burning!" Well, it didn't take her long to find out that the stove was red hot, and the soles of my shoes were beginning to smoke. She grabbed me away in a hurry and removed my shoes. Although my feet were beginning to feel hot, luckily I wasn't burned.
(Lauretta Cords)

Things had been going along smoothly for some time, when our teacher made the shocking announcement that from now on only English should be spoken on the playground. Uff da! What a headache! Did we have to use our company language even on the playground? Our household language was Norwegian, and that we enjoyed. It wasn't as if there were pupils who couldn't understand Norwegian. Every one of the forty pupils spoke it well. It wasn't that the teacher couldn't understand it either, because she did. We stormed about on the playground, declaring how downright unfair this new rule was to each and every one. The teacher had said that she thought American children should speak English while at school. We were patriotic, but this was carrying patriotism too far! When my mother heard the sad tale, she reacted calmly. "If you can talk Norwegian going to and from school, I am sure you will keep in trim," she said. Other parents must have taken it coolly as well. The threatened rebellion never took place.
(Ingeborg Bolstad)

We had a rule that no one was to leave the school grounds with-out permission. One day at noon, several of the older pupils took off without permission. They were even tardy for the opening of the one o'clock session. I thought that called for punishment, so I said that each of the offenders had to remain after school for one-half hour, especially since they wouldn't say where they had been. Classes proceeded, but with considerable tension. At about three-thirty,

several cars drove into the yard — out piled the mothers, laden with goodies for a picnic. The children had gone to a couple of homes to tell the mothers that it was my birthday and asked if they would bring the makings for a surprise party. Those mothers alerted the other mothers, and the result was a full-fledged party. No, the offenders did not have to stay an extra half hour!
(Mabel Winter)

It was December 1941, and all was in readiness for the afternoon performance of our Christmas program. The school was small, and parents and friends would have to come in the front door, across the stage, and go between the sheets which were used as curtains, before taking their place at desks in the back of the room. It was about one-thirty, with the program to start at two-thirty. The boys had been excused for a short time, and the girls were putting the finishing touches on the stage furnishings. The water fountain, which stood on a stand in the corner behind a sheet, had just been filled with water. When it was time for the boys to come back into the school, one lively ten-year-old came tearing in and crossed the room to get a drink. He couldn't stop in time and hit the fountain, overturning it, with about five gallons of icy water flooding the floor and soaking the hanging sheets. The boy was not hurt and the fountain did not break, but the frustrated teacher started to cry. What a mess! I sent some children to the neighbor's place for mops and more sheets. My landlady came to my rescue and brought extra sheets for curtains. She helped hang them, and after mopping up the water, we were pretty much ready for the program at two-thirty. The water fountain was not filled again until *after* the program. Santa Claus arrived on time with presents and candy, and the teacher regained her composure. Now I can smile when I meet that boy, grown to over six feet, who almost ruined the Christmas program.
(Kathleen Rietforts)

When I was in the sixth or seventh grade, we had terrible dust storms (the dust bowl days of the early 30s) that made our classroom so dark we could not see to do any work. Of course we had no lamps, etc., so we had to go home. I also remember that our Model T would choke up and die from all the dust in the engine.
(Mary D. Thompson)

It was in the Maker School that one of the practice teachers brought us scarlet fever. I got it, so was quarantined, as was customary to do then for contagious diseases. The local doctor gave me the word when I could go back to school. Someone saw the skin peeling off between my fingers, and one mother said that spread the disease. I had to get the doctor out to meet with those mothers and explain to them what they really *didn't* know about scarlet fever before they believed what I had told them.

Another time I had the doctor out to prove that some kids had impetigo. Most of the kids and I got that catchy stuff. I remember coming home when school was out in the spring and being banished to the attic with a complete cure or treatment to get rid of whatever I had before I could sleep in the beds or mingle with the rest of the family. Those were the days!
(Helen C. Williams)

Sadly to say, the death of a young child or baby was not uncommon in the days I attended school, and the family's grief was shared by the whole community. Funeral homes were not used at that time, so the visitation was always held at the family home. The teacher always spoke to the pupils about the tragedy, and then she and all the pupils would march, double file, from the school to the home of the bereaved, walk silently past the casket, and then back to school. This usually took about an hour, but it left a lifelong impression on everyone.
(Ida Posteher Fabyanske)

In one school, I opened the door one morning to find that the room was black dark. In a split second I knew what had happened. The oil burner had plugged up in some way and smoked until it burned out. There was no phone, so I had to get to a neighbor's house and let them know what had happened. There was no school that day or the next. The ladies in the district came to help clean up. No spot was left untouched by the soot. Even the books were smoke damaged.
(Signe Haraldson)

The schoolroom was heated by an old round stove that stood in the center of the room. It stood high on legs, and almost caused a disaster one time. One of the boys, who was being dragged by the teacher to the front of the room where he was to stand in the corner as punishment, hooked his foot behind a stove leg, pulling it down. Fortunately, there was no fire in the stove, but you should have seen the mess!
(Ruth V. Esping)

I had a first grader whose mother came for her after school was out each day. The first graders were let out at three-thirty to play in the yard until the older pupils got out. (I had six or seven classes of older ones in that half hour.) One day the first grader's mother came to the door to tell me her daughter wasn't waiting for her as usual, and we became alarmed. There were high cornfields on three sides of that schoolhouse, and I was afraid she'd gotten lost. So I sent my two big eighth-grade boys out to find her. They came back and reported that they had looked everywhere — even in the toilet holes! They couldn't find her anywhere. So I sent scouts out to track her route home, thinking maybe she had decided to walk home. They finally found her, hiding in a culvert with a boy, as a joke on her mother. Her mother had driven right over the culvert on her way to the school, and they had laughed and laughed.
(Elma Summers)

I remember one day sitting across the aisle from an older kid, say three or four years older than I. He had drawn a picture of a girl with no clothes on, and he passed it across the aisle for me to see. As I was passing it back to him, the teacher looked up and assumed that I had drawn the picture. Of course she didn't bother to ask. She told me to pass to the corner of the room. As I got up, the boy who had drawn the picture whispered to me, "Run for it." So that's what I did — straight to the outhouse! I got in and bolted the door with a 2 x 4 so the teacher couldn't get in. I waited until the teacher went back inside and then hightailed it for home. I told my parents about the episode, but was told I'd have to go back to school the next day to "face the music." When I came back, the teacher took my hand and slapped it with a ruler. I had a sore on that hand from a previous injury, and that now broke open. As it started to bleed, the teacher got a little worried about the action she had taken.
(David Wendell Hughes)

Opening day at school was quite chilly. The stove was the usual huge black hulk. I opened the door and saw that it was filled with scraps and waste paper. "Just enough to take off the chill," I thought. I threw in a match, and immediately a nice blaze erupted. But horrors! I realized, too late, that there were no stovepipes!! I almost panicked. I ran outdoors and was relieved to see one of the school board members driving in with his children. He told me to stay out;

he would take charge. Somehow he managed to put out the fire without it doing too much damage. He said that when a group had cleaned the schoolhouse, they decided also to clean the pipes, never thinking that the stove would be used on the first day of school. Luckily, I was not "fired."
(Mabel Winter)

How can I ever forget the morning in May when a thundershower came up and a bolt of lightning struck the schoolhouse. I think I never shall hear such a deafening sound again. First, we were just numb and couldn't move. When we got over being stunned, we got up and ran out of the schoolhouse — through a muddy field to a neighbor's place across the road. The family there was watching us, and they claimed there were splinters from the strike falling to the ground all around us as we ran; luckily, none hit us. The splinters came as a result of the lightning striking the roof of the schoolhouse and also the bell tower. The entry was moved inches away from the schoolhouse itself. The children's tin lunch boxes that sat on the floor in the entry were melted away — doughnuts, sandwiches, etc., burned and charred black. Needless to say, school was dismissed for the rest of the day.
(Lauretta Cords)

One of my first experiences after starting school in the fall of 1911 is maybe worth relating. There was no well on the school grounds, and water had to be carried from a neighbor's place. At one of the afternoon recesses, Sixten Swenson and I volunteered to fetch a pail of water from Magnuson's home. They had a large storage tank in the haymow of their barn; from there it flowed by gravity to the house, and was tapped from a faucet in the kitchen. This is where we got the water. When we returned to the school grounds, one of the older boys met us and spit in the pail of water. When we got inside with the water, we told what had happened. At once the teacher, Nancy Magnuson, stepped out on the porch and called this big boy to come forward. Then she asked Sixten and I what had happened. Sixten would not say anything (he was smarter than I — had started school the fall before in 1910). I told the teacher the facts and she made the boy empty the water pail, get it cleaned and go for another pail of water. For several weeks I hardly dared step outside of the school for fear of this big boy who was going to get even

with me for telling. I might add that I learned early that it doesn't pay to tattle on your friends.
(Holger O. Warner)

I think the first time I can remember going to school was as a guest of my older sister. It was not unusual to bring a younger brother or sister to school for a day. You shared the wood desk all day — all those wonderful books, a tablet of lined paper, and the smell of the wooden cedar pencils. It was always a very special treat to borrow the teacher's pencil. It seemed to be yellow, unchewed, had an eraser intact, and was long and well-sharpened. It felt clean, too. Being all of five years old, I noticed that the other students would get up and recite for the teacher. I heard a rooster crow off in the distance, so I stood up and did a very nice "cock-a-doodle-doo" for everyone, to their amusement and my sister's embarrassment. She never forgave me or took me along again!

Another time, I remember I had to stay after in first grade and write "get" on the blackboard (I had spelled it "git"). I had to write it a million times, it seemed, while my sister and brothers stood waiting, with their silent glare. I never had to stay after again!
(Jerrie Steinwall Ahrens)

I had a boy pupil who had grown to about six feet at grade school age. One day he got into a fight on the playground. When I saw the boys were fighting, I dashed out and got between them and sent them both in to their seats. When I later met up with a farmer who had been working in the field near the school, he laughed and told me how funny it was to see a little woman control those big boys!
(Edith O. Chaffer)

I had a little girl in the first grade who wouldn't read aloud; she would only whisper. She was a good reader and talked aloud in other classes. It went on like that for a month or more, when one day I asked her, "Virginia, will you read aloud for me if we send the pupils out to play?" Her answer was, "Yes." She started to read and was so pleased with herself. I stopped her and asked, "Shall we have Geraldine (her sister) come in to hear you read?" Again, her answer was, "Yes." It wasn't long before we had all the pupils back in the school listening to Virginia read aloud. What a happy little girl she now was!
(Marjorie Sperry)

One time in the school where I had twelve first graders, I had introduced the process of addition to them and most had gotten it right away. However, one little fellow just couldn't understand. I drew pictures, used objects, and things were getting pretty tight and heavy, since I was becoming very frustrated. The classroom was very quiet, and all the pupils were wondering what I was about to do to the poor little fellow. Finally I said, "Raymond, what is 1 + 1?" He replied with a pitiful look in his eye, "n-n-n-numbers." Needless to say, that broke the tension. I laughed, gave him a hug, and said, "Yes, Raymond, they are numbers." Everyone in the room laughed in relief. That was such a mistake; I should have realized that he just wasn't ready for addition.
(Margaret Thompson Cimenski)

The clothes we wore were simple. My brothers wore sweaters and knee pants — never, never jeans or overalls; that was for work in the fields. Poor as we were, that was a strict rule. My sister and I always wore dresses. We might have had two each, one for school and one for Sundays. The bloomers most always matched the dress, and there was a pocket on the front of the bloomers to carry a pretty hankie. Our stockings were heavy lisle, many times mended by spring, and in cold weather, the long underwear — yes, with the trap door! You were lucky if you had short sleeves on the underwear. Otherwise, you spent a lot of time tucking it up under your dress sleeve, pretending it didn't exist. I don't know why we were so concerned, because everyone wore it.

Shoes were practical brown oxfords, hand-me-downs, and worn until there were lovely holes in the leather soles. Then you could add a piece of cardboard for an inner lining, and when Daddy had time, he'd get his shoe-fixing tools out and repair the shoes himself. We had rubber gaiters and wool snow pants, coats, hats, and mittens. Snow stuck to everything, and once you went into a warm room, the snow on your clothes melted, the clothes got wet, and it was a while before you went out again. I remember my hands and wrists were always chapped to bleeding in the wintertime.
(Jerrie Steinwall Ahrens)

In the spring when the ground warmed up a little, nearly all of the boys and some of the girls went to school barefooted, and of course did not wear shoes during the summer vacation. So you can imagine the agony in the fall when the weather got cold and we had

to try to crowd our widened feet into the shoes we had set aside in the spring.
(Holger O. Warner)

The clothes worn on a cold winter's day consisted of one-piece long johns — better known as a "union suit" — cotton or wool socks, long shawls and heavy sweaters, petticoats, and skirts for the girls. We wore buckle boots over our shoes. The mothers usually made most of our clothes. I remember how much fun it was to go in to town to buy new long johns!
(Lucina E. Valento)

I remember wearing aprons over my dress to protect it — and wearing full, black, sateen bloomers. Also, I remember wearing long-legged underwear and trying to pull the long, ribbed stockings over them so they weren't bunchy. I wore bibbed blue overalls in the winter to further protect my legs. New ones faded and stained my stockings blue.
(Alice L. Soffa)

The following episode taught me a valuable lesson. A snowstorm had drifted the snow in the schoolyard in such a fashion that the schoolhouse appeared to be in a saucer. Since I was an inexperienced car driver, I didn't realize that the brakes were frozen until I tried to stop near the building. Since the only passable place to drive was around the building, I circled it three times without stopping, and then steered toward a snowbank. I didn't know I could have shut off the ignition! Anyway, I didn't stop until I hit the fence in front of the boys' toilet! One of my pupils asked, "Why didn't you stop where you always do, Miss Lambert?" Imagine my embarrassment when the wrecker men came to take the car to the garage from that location, and again when I had to report the damage to the school board clerk!
(Hannah Lambert)

I remember the Armistice Day snowstorm of 1940. It was in my teaching contract that school was to be in session on Armistice Day. I was at my boarding place, one-fourth mile from the country school, since my father took me there on Sunday afternoon. By seven-thirty on Monday morning, a school board member called and said that there would be no school that day. I didn't get to my country school until Wednesday afternoon, walking through snowdrifts up to my hips, since the gravel road had not been plowed out. There were snowdrifts in the schoolyard up to the steps and porch, and some snow had blown into the hall. I had to dig a path to the woodshed to get wood and coal, and then carry it into the schoolroom to build a fire in the large jacketed heating stove. After getting a fire built, I tramped through snowdrifts to try to check the outdoor toilets. There was snow packed solid above my head in the two toilets, as a result of the strong whipping winds of two and one-half days and nights.

I had school on Thursday, with one pupil present. By Friday I had gotten one toilet shoveled out so it could be used. I had seven pupils on Friday. The girls and boys took turns using the one toilet. On Friday at two o'clock, water started dripping from the ceiling onto the large dictionary toward the back of the room. Snow had blown into the attic and was starting to melt, after having heat in the schoolroom for two and one-half days. Drip! Drip! Drip! Yes, the dictionary was promptly moved!

(Orline Golden Foelschow)

A SPECIAL TOGETHERNESS

A SPECIAL TOGETHERNESS

A feeling of nostalgia often accompanies memories of the years spent teaching in a rural school. There was a togetherness or companionship there which was not found in other schoolrooms. If an older child got through with his lessons, he would, and did, help a younger sister, brother, or friend with his spelling, arithmetic, or reading.
(Dorothy Powell)

I still maintain that youngsters who attended a rural school had a special kind of education. We were like one big family. Everyone knew everyone else's hurts and problems, and showed their sympathy in many ways. They learned how to study on their own because most of their work was done by themselves. They "absorbed" much education, too, from listening to other classes that were reciting. We had some excellent students.
(Helen C. Williams)

The one thing that makes the country school special to me is the closeness that was felt between all of the students. There was also a certain closeness with the teachers. I had one teacher for grades one through four and then another for grades five through eight. Having the same teacher for so long gave me an opportunity to get to know each of them very well.
(Van Johnson)

When I was a child, people didn't go to town very often, and the country school was the center of community life. Neighborhood children would meet on the way to school and walk the long distance together. This provided for friendship and closeness. The Christmas program and box socials at Valentine's time brought the community together and were great fun. The Mothers' Club programs and lunches were also special times. Each one was happy when their mother attended.

I enjoyed everything about school and took it very seriously. Good grades and perfect attendance awards were important to me. And how I loved my first grade teacher! Recently, after so many years, we have resumed contact through an article I read about her in a Minneapolis newspaper.

There is much to be said about the goodness of that simple way of life. Surely, we were a healthy bunch — simple food and lots of exercise and fresh air!
(Mae Hanson Hughes Kjos)

I would like to say that rural schools were special. They provided a life-like situation. Children learned to share and to understand schoolmates of different ages. Honesty, self-discipline, patience, and respect were learned by close contact. It was necessary to work independently if one was to succeed. Neither money nor machines guarantee any better education. It's people who count. All in all, the rural school life is a time to remember. There is nothing else that can take its place. The rural school added much to our heritage. I am glad that I was able to participate. My earnest hope is that I gave a few, at least, a lift to a fulfilling life.
(Arlie M. Klimes)

I will always feel that the days spent in a rural school had something which could never be found in a city school. There was a closeness, togetherness, and friendship which brought everyone on an even basis. My four years of teaching are some of the happiest of my life, and my pupils will always remain very dear to me.
(Ada Ronnei Pederson)

To anyone not familiar with the excitement and trauma of being a pupil in District 11, our one-room school must have appeared prosaic. But to us who struggled over our "times tables" and went sliding on the "rubber ice" until someone broke through it, this was a place of laughter and tears, of challenges and surprises — the center of our lives. We who are products of District 11 treasure happy memories of the days we spent there. The friendships have been lasting, and some of the lessons have not been forgotten.
(Ingeborg Bolstad)

Country school was very special because all the people in our district knew each other and were involved in the programs, picnics, and box socials. There was a special togetherness — people caring about people.
(Elsie Fredericksen Williams)

I have many, many pleasant memories of my days of teaching, but perhaps the greatest reward came forty years after I quit teaching — on my eightieth birthday. Several of my friends and former pupils had a colossal idea. They went to the court house and got the names of all my former pupils and wrote to them, inviting them to come to an open house party or to write to me. What a thrill when the mailbox started filling with cards from all over the United States. I received about 150 beautiful cards and letters, and the church overflowed with former pupils and friends. That party climaxed an era of a life made full by country teaching and living.
(Mabel Winter)

As a farewell gift to me at the end of my four years of teaching, I was given a quilt. It was put together by the mothers, using the shirts and dresses of the children, and pieced together in blocks. What a precious reminder of the togetherness we shared.
(Ruby Vickers)

ACKNOWLEDGMENTS

I am deeply grateful to the following individuals for sending me their "Country School Memories." By taking the time to write down some of their recollections of country school life, that part of our heritage can now be preserved.

Ahrens, Jerrie Steinwall
— pupil, 1934-35, Dist. 1, Dakota Co., MN
Anderson, Clara
— teacher, 1927-45, Aitkin, Pope, and Swift Co., MN
Ball, Marva Rumelhart
— pupil, 1942-50, Budde School, Jerauld Co., Wessington Springs, SD
Barsness, Mabel
— pupil, 1907-17, Dist. 45, Pope Co., MN
Barsness, Olive
— teacher, 1918-26, Dist. 94, 52, and 88; Loury, Farwell, Kloten, ND
Bieberdorf, Ella
— pupil, 1913-20, Dist. 137, Hartford, SD
Block, Clarence
Bolstad, Ingeborg
— pupil, 1913-19, Dist. 11, Pope Co., MN
— teacher, 1924-28, Pope Co., MN
Brenden, Agnes
— pupil, 1909-18, Blue Mounds Township, Dist. 42, MN
— teacher, 1923-48, Pope and Kandiyohi Co., MN
Burtness, Hannah
— teacher, Waseca Co., MN, 3 years; Freeborn Co., MN, 25 years
Campbell, Viola Burnett
— teacher, 1935-39, Nicollet and Judson, MN
Chaffer, Edith O.
— pupil, 1912-20, Ten Mile School, E. Peoria, IL
— teacher, 1925-36, various rural schools near E. Peoria, Mackinaw, and Morton, IL
Cimenski, Margaret Thompson
— pupil, 1920-28, Dist. 3, Crow Wing Co., Brainerd, MN

— teacher, 1934-55, various rural schools in Crow Wing Co., MN

Cords, Lauretta
— pupil, 1904-12, Grams School, Blue Earth Co., MN

Cummings, Frances E.
— pupil, 1921-29, Wolverine and Imlay City, MI

Cummings, Wallie D.
— pupil, 1910-18, Huckins School, Croswell, MI

Delage, Deloris
— pupil, 1940-47, Poplar River School, Brooks, MN

Demuth, Ann

Esping, Ruth V.
— pupil, 1909-17, Dist. 55
— teacher, 1924- (11 years), Dist. 55, 24, and 35, MN

Fabyanske, Ida Posteher
— pupil, 1920-27, McCarron's Lake School, Dist. 29, MN

Foelschow, Orline Golden
— pupil, 1925-31, Dist. 74, Swift Co., Milan, MN
— teacher, 1939-41, Dist. 64, Swift Co., Benson, MN; 1945-46, Dist. 74, Swift Co., Milan, MN

Fredericksen, N. Wyelene
— pupil, 1920-28, Maker School, Lincoln Township, Blue Earth Co., MN

Hagedorn, Clara G.
— teacher, 1935-37, Willow Lawn School, Clay Co., IA

Hanson, Pat
— pupil, 1935-40, Honeyford, ND
— teacher, 1949-50, Walcott, ND

Haraldson, Signe
— pupil, 1912-18, Rock and Pipestone Co., MN
— teacher, taught 31 years in all

Hardin, Mae F.
— pupil, 1924-30, Royal School #1, Starkweather, ND

Hauge, Sophie C. Vold
— pupil, 1914-22, Dist. 87, Pope Co., Glenwood, MN
— teacher, 1928-29, Dist. 9, Pope Co., Glenwood, MN; 1929-30, Dist. 24, Pope Co., Sedan, MN; 1932-36, Dist. 37, Pope Co., Starbuck, MN

Hedlund, Margaret Seeger
— pupil, 1925-33, Minnesota and North Dakota
— teacher, 1938-41, Dist. 73, Pope Co., MN

Hughes, David Wendell
— pupil, 1908-16, Dist. 11, Cambria, MN
Hughes, Selma Anderson
— pupil, 1918-26, Dist. 122, Blue Earth Co., MN
— teacher, 1932-38, Dist. 78 and 11, Blue Earth Co., MN
Jeddeloh, Carol Johnston
Jenkins, Alice M.
— pupil, 1927-32, Horeb School, Cambria, MN
Jenkins, Margaret
— pupil, 1927-33, Dist. 11, Cambria, MN
Johansen, Ruth Aleda
— teacher, 1920-23, Four Mile Creek School and Long
Lake School in rural Northern Wisconsin
Johnson, Blanche Lindholm
— teacher, 1917-23, McPherson Co., KS; 1930-31, Saline
Co., KS
Johnson, Milton S.
— pupil, 1918-26, Dist. 36, Lincoln Co., SD
Johnson, Van
— pupil, 1942-50, Dist. 139, Browerville, MN
Jones, Roland H.
— pupil, 1905-16, Llanfairfechan, North Wales
Juhl, Elizabeth
— pupil, 1901-09, near Fenton, IA
Kjos, Mae Hanson Hughes
— pupil, Lincoln Township, Blue Earth Co., MN
Klimes, Arlie M.
— teacher, 1927-71, Nobles, Rock, and Pipestone Co., MN
Lambert, Hannah
— teacher, 40+ years in Waseca and Steele Co., and
Madelia, North Mankato, and Faribault, MN
McKinley, Ethelyn
— pupil, 1911-16, Waseca Co., Waseca, MN
McKinley, Forrest
— pupil, 1907-16, Dist. 162, Stearns Co., Paynesville, MN
Meixell, Reba Clark
— teacher, 1926-31, Dist. 119, South Lincoln, and Dist. 92,
Good Thunder, MN
Nannestad, Eldora
— pupil, 1911-17, Sherburne Co., MN
— teacher, 1924-53, Douglas, Sherburne, Pipestone, and
Rock Co., MN

Norton, Mary Ann

Oldenborg, Harley
- pupil, 1921-30, Lake Benton, Marshfield, Lincoln Co., MN

Olson, Frances Crook
- pupil, 1917-18, Pleasant View, Blue Earth Co., MN
- teacher, 1931-45, four schools in Blue Earth Co., MN

Ose, Sally L.
- pupil
- teacher, taught 29 years in various rural schools

Parquet, Hazel Hubbart
- pupil, 1929-35, Manley School, Beaver Township, Miner Co., SD
- teacher, 1944-48, Manley School, Beaver Township, Miner Co., SD

Pederson, Ada Ronnei
- pupil, 1913-21, Dist. 45, Pope Co., MN
- teacher, 1927-31, Dist. 90, Pope Co., MN

Powell, Dorothy
- teacher, 12 years in Steele and Waseca Co., MN

Quissell, Mrs. Julian
- teacher, 1939-41, Quissell Country School, Moody Co., SD

Rietforts, Kathleen
- teacher, Kilkenny Co., Nebraska; Waseca and Steele Co., MN

Sanvik, Selma O.
- pupil, 1917-25, Dist. 44, Pope Co., MN
- teacher, 1930-41, Pope and Stevens Co., MN

Schlichter, Norma Hughes
- pupil, 1947-52, Maker School, Blue Earth Co., MN

Sedlacek, Emily
- pupil, 1920-26, Dist. 29, Moody Co., Ward, SD
- teacher, 1931-56, Dist. 19, 69, 64, 62, 36, 9, 12, 46, 73

Siefkes, Lucille
- pupil, 1926-29, Dist. 162, Andover, SD

Soffa, Alice L.
- pupil, 1924-31, Clear Grit
- teacher, 1936-45, Larson, Watson Creek, Brokken, Zion, Maple Lane, Clear Grit

Sperry, Marjorie
— pupil, 1910-11, in rural school
— teacher, 1927-30, in rural school
Studt, Lorena
Summers, Elma
— teacher, 1941-50, Butternut, Maker School, Helleckson
School, Watonwan School, MN

Thompson, Dorothea
— pupil, 1918-24, Hardwick, MN
— teacher, 1931-69, Rock, Pipestone, and Nobles Co., MN;
and Lyon Co., IA
Thompson, Mary D.
— pupil, 1928-36, Hanson 25-1 and Hanson 25-2 and
Ferney, SD
— teacher, 1941-43, Hanson 25-1 (south of Groton, SD)

Valento, Lucina E.
— pupil, 1923-29, Richmond, MN
Vickers, Ruby
— pupil, 1916-23, Huffton, SD
— teacher, 1927-31, Barnes School, Claremont, SD

Waite, Magdalene
— pupil, 1914-20, Trosky, MN
— teacher, 1926-59, Dist. 13, Hatfield, MN; Dist. 51,
Trosky, MN; Dist. 17 and 24, Pipestone Co., MN
Warner, Holger O.
— pupil, 1911-19, Dist. 33, Fish Lake Township, Chisago
Co., MN
Williams, Elsie S. Fredericksen
— pupil, 1923-31, Maker School, Dist. 89, MN
Williams, Helen C.
— teacher, 1925-72, Yellow Medicine Co., Judson, and
Blue Earth Co., MN
Wilson, Diann Lundeby
— pupil, 1952-59, Mission #2 School, Devils Lake, ND
Winter, Mabel
— pupil, 1910-17, Dist. 52, Traverse Co., Wheaton, MN
— teacher, 1922-41, various rural schools in Traverse Co.,
MN

This book evolved from a project I started in an American Folklore class at Lakewood Community College several years ago. I would like to thank John Schell, my folklore instructor, for his inspiration.

I would like to thank the following individuals and organizations for providing me with sources for this book and helping me in various other ways.

INDIVIDUALS: Marian Anderson, Ken Brauns, Allan F. Degnan, Dawn Blair Gullickson, Mary Hilke, Janet Huber, Vicki A. Johnson, Sherry Jones, Peggy Korsmo-Kennon, Robert Kuehn, Darlene Lenard, Minnie Osterholt, Shirley Selzer, Diane Skelnik, Terri Snider, Gail Westby, and Bertha Zniewski.

A special thank you to Nick Cords for his valuable advice, support, and encouragement.

I would also like to thank my husband, Tom, and sons, Scott and Andy, for their patience and understanding while I worked on this book.

HISTORICAL SOCIETIES: Cass County, Dakota County, Douglas County, Fillmore County, Koochiching County, Mille Lac Lake, Paynesville County, Pipestone County, Pope County, and Waseca County.

The Minnesota Historical Society was a valuable resource for researching the history of one-room schools in Minnesota.

ABOUT THE ILLUSTRATOR

Nancy Delage Huber graduated from the University of Minnesota — Morris, with majors in studio art and biology. She has been drawing since she was a small child, and now specializes in pen and ink illustration.

Nancy and her husband currently live in the Twin Cities area, where she works as a graphic designer.

ABOUT THE AUTHOR

In 1951, I attended first grade in a country school in southern Minnesota. It was called the Maker School and is located in Lincoln Township, Blue Earth County. At the end of that school year, the school district was consolidated, and I attended grades two through twelve in Lake Crystal, Minnesota.

Although I only attended a country school for one year, I have many pleasant memories revolving around that little building. Through the years, it has been used for Farm Bureau meetings, 4-H Club meetings, elections, box socials, potlucks, bridal showers, etc. When I was in the seventh grade, I even hosted a class party there for all my "city friends." The schoolhouse, which is located about one-half mile from the farm where I grew up, is still standing and is now called the Lincoln Township Hall.

I currently live in White Bear Lake, Minnesota, with my husband and two teen-age sons. I enjoy writing about everyday people and events. I specialize in researching and recording stories and events of the past—preserving our heritage. By integrating the fields of journalism, history, folklore, and design, I facilitate others in telling their stories. This is the second book I have published. My first book, *Forget-Me-Not*, is a collection of verses written in autograph albums from the 1880s to the present.

Bonnie Hughes Falk

My first day of school
1951

The above photographs were taken about 1948–1950 at the Maker School, located in Lincoln Township, Blue Earth County, Minnesota. In the middle photo, I'm the little one on the left, with my sister Norma standing behind me. (It must have been visiting day!)

"*Country School Memories* fascinated me, and I read it almost from cover to cover without putting it down.

The one-room school was a significant phase in our American culture, and Bonnie Hughes Falk has rendered us all a service by assembling and publishing these anecdotes of country school life."

—Dr. H. Conrad Hoyer

"My children are enjoying their copies of *Country School Memories*, and my grandchildren are learning (and laughing!) about the way things were when grandma was young."

—Margaret Seeger Hedlund

"In a unique and entertaining format, Bonnie Hughes Falk has brought us nostalgic recollections of a way of life that today exist only in our childhood memories.

Bonnie is to be commended for her outstanding effort in recording and preserving an important part of our heritage!"

—Allan F. Degnan

A GREAT GIFT FOR

- a former classmate or teacher
- a "special" relative or friend
- your local senior citizen center or library

ORDER FORM

Send orders to: Bonnie Hughes Falk
BHF Memories Unlimited
3470 Rolling View Court
White Bear Lake, MN 55110
(612) 770-1922

Price is $9.45 (includes postage, handling, and tax)
Make checks payable to: Bonnie Hughes Falk

I have enclosed $_____ for ____ book(s). Send it/them to:

Name _____

Street_____

City _____ State _____ Zip _____